ROUTLEDGE LIBRARY EDITIONS: THE ECONOMY OF THE MIDDLE EAST

Volume 17

LIBYA SINCE INDEPENDENCE

LIBYA SINCE INDEPENDENCE
Economic and Political Development

Edited by
J. A. ALLAN

LONDON AND NEW YORK

First published in 1982

This edition first published in 2015
by Routledge
2 Park Square, Milton Park, Abingdon, Oxon, OX14 4RN

and by Routledge
711 Third Avenue, New York, NY 10017

Routledge is an imprint of the Taylor & Francis Group, an informa business

© 1982 J.A. Allan

All rights reserved. No part of this book may be reprinted or reproduced or utilised in any form or by any electronic, mechanical, or other means, now known or hereafter invented, including photocopying and recording, or in any information storage or retrieval system, without permission in writing from the publishers.

Trademark notice: Product or corporate names may be trademarks or registered trademarks, and are used only for identification and explanation without intent to infringe.

British Library Cataloguing in Publication Data
A catalogue record for this book is available from the British Library

ISBN: 978-1-138-78710-0 (Set)
eISBN: 978-1-315-74408-7 (Set)
ISBN: 978-1-138-81177-5 (Volume 17)
eISBN: 978-1-315-74632-6 (Volume 17)
Pb ISBN: 978-1-138-82020-3 (Volume 17)

Publisher's Note
The publisher has gone to great lengths to ensure the quality of this reprint but points out that some imperfections in the original copies may be apparent.

Disclaimer
The publisher has made every effort to trace copyright holders and would welcome correspondence from those they have been unable to trace.

Libya
Since Independence
ECONOMIC AND POLITICAL DEVELOPMENT

Edited by J.A. Allan

CROOM HELM   London & Canberra
ST. MARTIN'S PRESS   New York

© 1982 J.A. Allan
Croom Helm Ltd, Provident House, Burrell Row,
Beckenham, Kent BR3 1AT

British Library Cataloguing in Publication Data

Libya since independence.
   1. Libya — Economic conditions
 I. Allan, J.A.
 330.961'204   HC567.L5
 ISBN 0-7099-0519-X

All rights reserved. For information write:
St. Martin's Press, Inc., 175 Fifth Avenue, New York, N. Y. 10010

First published in the United States of America in 1982

Library of Congress Cataloging in Publication Data
Main entry under title:

Libya since independence.

   1. Libya — Economic policy — Addresses, essays,
lectures. I. Allan, J. A. (John Anthony)
HC825.L5217   1982   338.961'2   82-42564
ISBN 0-312-48363-5

The chapters of this book have been based
on a selection of the papers presented at
a conference held in London in July 1981.
The papers not reproduced here appear in
a companion volume edited by E.G.H. Joffe
and K.S. McLachlan entitled Social and
Economic Development of Libya since 1835,
published by Menas Press Limited, London,
in 1982.

Printed and bound in Great Britain

CONTENTS

List of figures ii

Foreword and Acknowledgements iii

Note on Transliteration of Placenames iv

PART ONE: RESOURCE USE AND ECONOMIC DEVELOPMENT

1 Natural Resource Use: Lessons from the Past
  Graeme Barker 3

2 Strategies for Agricultural Development in Libya
  Keith McLachlan 9

3 Capital Has Not Substituted for Water in Agriculture
  Tony Allan 25

4 Development of the Libyan Oil Industry
  Paul Barker and Keith McLachlan 37

5 The Development of Libyan Industry
  Paul Barker 55

6 The Libyan Fishing Industry
  Ewan Anderson and Gerald Blake 73

7 Transport and Investment in the Libyan Jamahiriya 1963-1980
  Abulgasim Elazzabi 93

PART TWO: ASPECTS OF SOCIAL AND POLITICAL DEVELOPMENT

8 Cultural and Social Diversity in Libya
  Emrys Peters 103

9 The Political Development of Libya 1952-1969: Institutions, Policies and Ideology
  Salaheddin Hasan Sury 121

10 The Green Book: Its Context and Meaning
   Hervé Bleuchot 137

11 Frontiers: an Imported Concept: an Historical Review of the Creation and Consequences of Libya's Frontiers
   Martine Muller 165

Index

LIST OF FIGURES

1	The Study Area of the Valleys Survey	2
2	Water Development Regions and Agricultural Development Areas	27
3	Water Resource Development 1950-2000, by Region and Type of Use	28
4	Forecast Oil Production and Domestic Oil Consumption in Libya 1979-1990	36
5	Western Libya: Fishing Ports, Tonnaras and Sponge Limits	91
6	Libya's Road Network 1950-1979	92
7	Administrative Divisions of Libya pre-1969	136
8	Border Agreements and Disputed Borders	180

FOREWORD AND ACKNOWLEDGEMENTS

The changes effected in Libya's economy, society and political systems since oil figured as an element in the economy and the country embarked on ambitious policies based on oil-wealth after the 1969 revolution though dramatic have not been comprehensively documented. A meeting was held in July 1981 in the University of London at the Centre for Middle Eastern Studies, School of Oriental and African Studies to bring together specialists in Libyan affairs as well as historians of the late nineteenth and twentieth centuries.

The chapters assembled in this volume are concerned with the period since independence in 1951 and examine all the important elements of the economy and some of its major sectors such as transport. The political organisation of the period of the monarchy is reviewed and analysed in terms of its institutions, policies and ideology and the political experiments of the revolutionary period are critically examined with special reference to *The Green Book* of Mu'ammar al Qadhafi. Finally there is a discussion of Libya's frontiers and their origins, and this material has been included because although Libyan international interests have been wide ranging since 1969, her real external interests are to extend her natural resource base and much that has occurred in the recent past and that which happens in the future will be based on Libya's perception of her territorial entitlement.

The assistance of the Society for Libyan Studies in covering some of the expenses of the conference and of universities and research institutions in Libya and elsewhere in facilitating the attendance of participants is gratefully acknowledged.

The material selected for this volume covers

Foreword and Acknowledgements

the socio-economic and political changes experienced since independence. The papers not included in this volume dealt mainly with the economic and social history of Libya in the nineteenth and early twentieth centuries and they have been published in a companion volume edited by E G H Joffé and K S McLachlan entitled, *Social and economic development of Libya since 1835*, published by Menas Press Ltd, London, 1982.

The editor is grateful to the contributors for their cooperation and assistance and especially to Mr Paul Barker and Dr Keith McLachlan for undertaking additional writing in order to improve the balance of the economic section of the book, to Mr George Joffé for the translation of the chapters by Dr Hervé Bleuchot and Ms Martine Muller, and to Ms Liz Johnson for the preparation of diagrams and the cartography of the maps.

The assistance of the Society for Libyan Studies in covering some of the expenses of the conference and of the universities and research institutions in Libya and elsewhere in facilitating the attendance of participants is gratefully acknowledged. These contributions made the conference possible and have enabled the publication of this and a companion volume. The opinions expressed in the book are those of the contributors and they are not necessarily held by staff and officials of the sponsoring institutions, the Centre of Middle Eastern Studies of the School of Oriental and African Studies and The Society for Libyan Studies.

JAA

Note on Transliteration of Placenames and Other Terms

Names of places falling in Libya have generally been transliterated according to the system of the US Board on Geographic Names, 1958, *Gazetteer No 41, Libya*, Washington DC. Names of places outside Libya have been rendered according to the convention most familiar for such places, usually the French system. As the chapters have been provided by authors from a number of different countries, Arabic words have been rendered in the form familiar to the author. In addition in the chapter on the oil industry placenames have been shown in a form generally familiar in the oil industry.

PART 1

RESOURCE USE
AND
ECONOMIC DEVELOPMENT

Natural resource use: lessons from the past

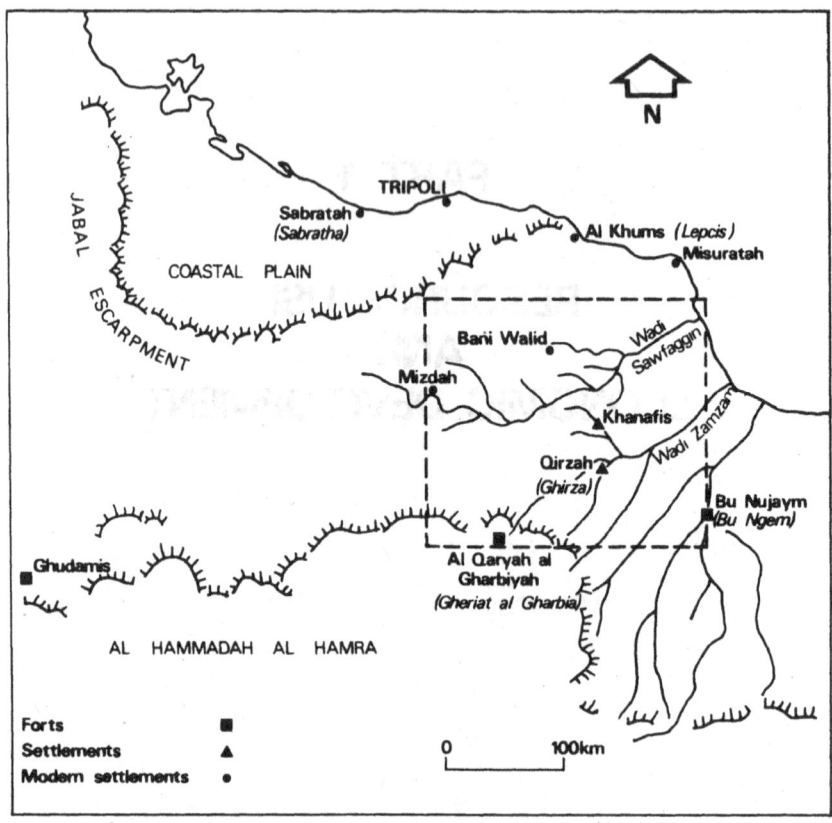

Figure 1. The study area of the Valleys Survey. The sites being investigated were farmed in the Romano Libyan period.

Chapter 1
NATURAL RESOURCE USE: LESSONS FROM THE PAST

G. Barker

Although archaeology is so often portrayed as the study of past cultural achievement through fine artifacts, monumental buildings and so on, the purpose of this paper is to illustrate another kind of archaeology - far less spectacular, but one which is, I submit, of considerable importance for modern Libya: the analysis of past societies and land use.

The preferred zone of settlement in Tripolitania has traditionally been the well watered coastal plain and the adjacent limestone hills of the Tarhunah Jabal as far south as the town of Bani Walid, for these regions have more than 200mm of rain a year, regarded as the threshold for settled farming without irrigation. Prehistoric settlement concentrated here, and mixed farming has probably characterised this zone from the fourth millennium BC. In the Roman period the coastal cities like Sabratha and Leptis Magna were supported by prosperous farms on the plain and in the Jabal. In the Islamic period, too, the same region was densely settled. In his journey through Libya over a century ago Heinrich Barth found here a rich and densely settled land 'adorned by numbers of beautiful olive trees and enlivened by small villages'.[1]

South of Bani Walid, however, the country changes rapidly. Barth described the stoney wastes of the arid pre-desert plateau very aptly as a 'sea-like level of desolation'. The plateau is dissected by the enormous wadi system of the Sawfaggin and Zam Zam. The main wadis are huge troughs filled with sheets of alluvial gravels and impassable dunes; the subsidiary wadis are normally narrow trenches covered by flood loams. Rainfall decreases very rapidly south of Bani Walid, to less than 25mm, causing sporadic but ferocious flash floods in the autumn and spring. The traditional system of land

Natural resource use: lessons from the past

use adapted to this environment is one of semi-nomadic pastoralism. Barth describes such a system in the last century: there was a dispersed population, who grew small stands of barley in the wadi loams, and who kept large flocks of goats, sheep, and to a lesser extent camels. Most of them summered in the Sawfaggin and Zam Zam area, but wintered on the desert margin to the south. Before modern technology enabled the construction of deep wells, water for animals and men had to be conserved in rock-cut cisterns. Prehistoric and Islamic land use in the pre-desert was probably much like the semi-nomadism described by Barth, although the evidence for this will not be cited in this chapter. What is clear, however, is that there was a much denser pattern of settlement in this region at some time in the Roman period.

Barth was the first to describe systematically frequent stone 'castles' on the wadi edges, often associated with evidence for cultivation in the form of 'broad and firmly constructed dikes.. built of small stones' running across the narrower tributary wadis at frequent intervals. There was a group of particularly massive 'castles' associated with 'ancient sepulchres' at Ghirza 100 kms south of Bani Walid in an area of minimal rainfall. Clearly the evidence suggested that the desolate plateau had once supported a very different pattern of agricultural settlement. Systematic archaeological study of these remains by Goodchild and Brogan in the 1950s and 1960s suggested that they were late Roman in date, probably of the third century AD and later.[2][3][4][5]

Such a date coincides with historical references to Roman imperial frontier policy advocating the use of army veterans as soldier-farmers (limitanei) in sensitive frontier areas. Hence Goodchild argued that the distribution of the 'castles' (now known from the Arabic *gsur*), extending for some 200 kms from west to east and for some 150 kms from north to south, represented a massive and elaborate system of frontier defence for the Roman empire, as well as an intensive system of land use very different from that of recent times. However, nothing was known in detail of the nature of this farming system, although the classical authors tell us that North Africa generally was considered the granary of Rome, and many of the coastal cities certainly exported grain and other foodstuffs to Rome, presumably from their hinterlands.

The Unesco Libyan Valleys Survey was initiated

in 1979 in order to gain more precise understanding
of the ancient farming system as an aid to planning
agricultural development in the same area in the
future. A major problem of previous research on
ancient settlement in Libya has been the separation
of disciplines and research goals; the historian
has argued from his sources; the prehistorians has
discussed culture history from artifact scatters and
cave sites; the Roman archaeologist has planned and
recorded *gsur*, primarily to answer chronological
questions; the geomorphologist has studied alluvial
phases near the coast, sometimes associated with
buried archaeological sites. Secondly, most archaeological fieldwork has been vehicle-based and extensive, rather than intensive and on foot. Given the
need therefore, for integrated and detailed information, the research strategy of the Valleys Survey
has been based on the interdisciplinary analysis of
small study areas selected at different points in a
north/south transect across the region from Bani
Walid to south of Ghirza. The strategy has been
designed to tackle six main questions. What was the
nature of the *gsur* settlement system and how did the
agricultural system associated with it function?
Why did it begin and why did it end? What were the
climatic/environmental conditions in which it flourished and ended and could or should the Roman farming experiment be repeated? I shall consider these
six questions in turn.[6]

First, what was the nature of the settlement
system? Two main categories of Roman site were
known in the area prior to the survey - the *gasr* and
the obelisk. However, we have found that there was
in fact a complex hierarchy of domestic and funerary
archaeology, with the *gasr* and the obelisk at the
top: below the *gasr* were large enclosures with
buildings, small enclosures with buildings, isolated
huts with pens, and isolated huts; below the
obelisk was a series of cairn types. The major sites
are by the wadi edge, but the others can extend
several kilometres onto the pateau, quite invisible
to normal vehicle survey. All these sites invari-
ably cluster along the narrower wadis and are
associated with wadi walls; in the wider wadis
there are no walls or *gsur*, but there are often
enclosed hilltop villages. The pottery associated
with all the sites indicates a date range earlier
than expected, from the first to the third centuries
AD.

Secondly, how did the agricultural system
function? Analysis of the wadi walls has revealed

complex systems of water and soil management, based on detailed local knowledge of water flows and soil distribution. Flood waters on the plateau edge were directed by side walls and culverts down to the wadi floor: here, other walls were built to control, narrow or widen the flow; still others formed land divisions unrelated to water flow, and stock enclosures. On the plateau, too, flood waters were directed by other wall systems into shallow silty depressions to improve grazing and browse. From variations in wall technology, in settlement forms, in soil distributions, and from botanical samples from Ghirza, we argue that the agricultural system was broadly based, and probably included the cultivation of olives, vines, figs and barley, but emphasised particularly the rearing of sheep and goats. At the same time, there was a broad geographical trend from north to south, with pastoralism increasing and arboriculture decreasing in importance moving south. However, there were also differences between adjacent wadis and even within wadis that are not simply a function of locational factors.

Thirdly why did the *gsur* agricultural system begin? We have found that many of the smaller domestic and funerary structures are identical to those of the late prehistoric period. At the same time epigraphic evidence indicates that most *gsur* were in fact built by local Libyan people rather than by Romans. These two lines of evidence, together with the fact that agricultural rather than defensive considerations dominate most site locations, suggest very strongly that most of the archaeology represents an internal process of social and economic transformation, with most *gsur* being built as outward-looking symbols of indigenous wealth and power rather than as colonial fortified farms of *limitanei*. (Pottery dating also suggests that *gsur* developed rather later than the enclosure farms). A number of models to account for this process can be put forward, but the most likely explanation is that a more intensive agricultural system capable of a modest surplus was developed by local chieftans in response to the economic pressure of the Roman coastal market. Something of the complexity of the process, however, can be seen in the Wadi Nufayd: in the centre was Qasr Banat, perhaps a Roman fort of the classic *limitanei* model; in the middle wadi were pastoral-based villages in the wider sections and mixed farming communities in the narrower sections; and at either end, where communications to the coast were easier, were large olive farms, perhaps colonial establishments.

Natural resource use: lessons from the past

The fourth and fifth questions relate to the reasons why the *gsur* systems ended and in what climatic/environmental conditions it flourished and ended. These questions have been less thoroughly investigated, however, preliminary studies of soil sections associated with wadi walls have thus far indicated that the main phase of farming and wall building took place in the same environment seen today of flood loams and dune sands. On the other hand, other sections in side wadis have provided evidence for phases of erosion on the plateau of a richer soil than is currently available, somewhere between the early classical period and the present (radiocarbon determinations are in progress). At the moment, however, we cannot tell whether these erosional episodes were caused by man, climate, or both, nor even whether they are related chronologically to the collapse of *gsur* farming. If they are not, then the most likely explanation for the event (and it is not yet clear if the settlement collapse was synchronous between the various wadis or between the various categories of site) probably lies in socio-economic changes in the relationship between this region and the coastal population. A great deal more information is needed about soil history in each part of our study area, both within and outside the settled areas.

Finally, could or should the Roman farming experiment be repeated? Any comment on the long term feasibility of agricultural development in the pre-desert of north-western Libya will clearly depend on the models we develop for the preceding questions. However, what is at least clear thus far is that the evident success of the earlier system of farming two thousand years ago depended above all on a detailed local knowledge of water and soil, and the fact that the production strategy of each farming unit was geared to local resources and constraints and not to any large scale plan. Secondly, our preliminary calculations from the settlement archaeology and cistern capacities indicate very modest population levels and herd sizes: most of the system consisted of traditional subsistence policies improved in degree rather than kind to produce a modest surplus, not a vastly intensified market economy. Thirdly, our opinion is that much of the wall building and water control was primarily to improve grazing land for sheep and goats rather than arable farming. In the long term, the traditional system of subsistence pastoralism has certainly been a more successful adaptation to the pre-desert environment than the experiment of the late Roman period, although modern technology is such that it may well be possible to circumvent the failures of that experiment. The study is only just beginning to get to grips with the crucial problem of why this agricultural system collapsed, but it seems evident already that a crucial part of future agricultural planning in Libya should be the archaeological perspective.

Notes

1. Barth, H., 1857, *Travels and Discoveries in North and Central Africa*, Longman, London pp 450
2. Brogan, O., and Smith, D.E. 1957, The Roman frontier settlement at Ghirza: an interim report, *Journal of Roman Studies*, 47: 173-184
3. Goodchild, R.G., 1950, The Limes Tripolitanus II, *Journal of Roman Studies*, 40: 30-38
4. Goodchild, R.G., 1951, Roman sites on the Tarhuna plateau of Tripolitania, *Papers of the British School at Rome*, 19: 43-65
5. Goodchild, R.G., 1976, *Libyan Studies: Selected Papers of the late R.G. Goodchild* (edited by J Reynolds), Elek, London
6. Jones, G.G.D., and Barker, G., 1979-1980, The Libyan Valleys Survey, *Libyan Studies*, 11,11-36

Acknowledgements

The work discussed here was possible as a result of a study funded and organised via UNESCO for the Libyan Department of Antiquities under the direction of Dr Abdullah Shaiyboub. The research discussed was supervised by the author and Professor G D B Jones on behalf of the Department, UNESCO and the Society for Libyan Studies.

Chapter 2
STRATEGIES FOR AGRICULTURAL DEVELOPMENT IN LIBYA

K.S.McLachlan

INTRODUCTION

Appropriate strategies for agricultural development in Libya have never been easy to elaborate. Constraints on agricultural activities arising from severe enviromental problems apply throughout the country, being only slightly less constricting in the north than in the south. Poverty of basic land and water resources is well documented[1] and needs no further examination here. Effects of adverse natural conditions are demonstrated in a UNDP assessment of land use in Libya summarized in Table 1.
    The concern of the ruling authorities in Libya during the present century has largely been with the arable and orchard farming, comprising a mere 1.1 per cent of the country's land surface. Some lip-service has been paid from time to time to the potential in the grazing areas though few concerted programmes of development have been formulated.[2] Even fewer have been implemented. The bulk of the so-called wastelands have always been regarded as outside the ambit of serious agriculture. A deep and continuing discrepancy between the perceptions of the planners and the reality of actual activities by the Libyan population in the use of the pasturelands and the wastlands has generally been ignored. Despite oil wealth and a diminution in the employment role of agriculture as a whole, the pastoral-shifting cultivation tradition has been maintained outside the arable and orchard farming zone making nonsense of the notion that such areas are 'wastelands' and serving as a reproach to ignorance of the planners concerning the potential still inherent in this 94.57 per cent of the country.

Strategies for Agricultural Development in Libya

Table 1: Land Use

Land use type	Area km^2	% total area
Urban	500	0.03
Agriculture - arable and orchard	18,000	1.10
Agriculture - pasture and grassland	70,000	4.00
Forest and scrubland	5,000	0.30
Wastelands	1,666,000	94.57
Total	1,760,000	100.00

Source: National Physical Perspective Plan 1981-2000, UNDP, Tripoli, March 1979, p 36

    The cleavage between concentrated agricultural activity in the northern coastal districts and diffuse and barely recognized use of the land in the south (outside the oasis areas) poses special problems for Libya. A dichotomy between populated, urbanized and economically productive coast and empty interior is typical of the Maghreb as a whole. To the extent that unpopulated territory can be deemed to be vulnerable to encroachments from outside, Libya's land use pattern gives rise to problems of a political nature. Certainly up to 1935 the tenuous command structure imposed over Libya by the Ottoman and later Italian authorities permitted, even encouraged, neighbouring states to lay successful claim to border areas.[3] It must be accepted at the outset, therefore, that experience in the recent past has created a measure of political imperative within the framework of agricultural planning. Whether such political considerations should be accommodated in so crude and expensive a form as the development of agricultural production and settlement projects such as al Kufrah and Sarir is to be questioned. Alternative means of achieving similar national political objectives are feasible and more adjusted to local requirements.[4]

    Historical pressures are to be seen, too, in the fact that strategies for development in Libya were mainly dictated from outside until recently. In particular, the Italian colonial administration left a deep imprint on the agricultural landscape, the style of land use and the location of farming activity. Temporary seizure of rule in Libya by the British and French during and after the Second World War did little to change the impact of the Italian pattern of agricultural development. One imaginative outline of land use that sought to redress the balance for indigenous as opposed to Italian farmers prepared by Rowland and Robb in the 1940s was never put into practice by the British Military Administration. In retaining its statutory responsibilities for 'care and maintenance' as occupying power, the BMA allowed the opportunity to pass for a radical shift in Tripolitania from colonially to locally oriented agricultural development.

Yet the Italian mode of development that affected Tripolitania so strongly and influenced other parts of the country in lesser degree was devised for a unique political situation, in which Libya functioned as a prospectively integral part of the metropolitan country.[5] Economically, Libya was a satellite of Italy, its agriculture subsidized and above all utilized as a tool for the settlement of Italian families, the aim of which was political rather than economic. Regardless of the artificial political and economic regimes in which they were set up, Italian colonial agricultural patterns have remained superimposed on Libya. While in some ways there was much that was admirable in Italian dedication to agricultural expansion in Libya, its physical form has been a mixed legacy, often acting as a strait-jacket impeding both adoption of new conceptions of strategies for agriculture and also introduction of more appropriate agrarian structures.

LIBYAN AGRICULTURE BEFORE OIL - 1951 TO 1961

The care and maintenance policies of the Military Administration in Libya, in which the occupying powers sought to minimize their expenses in fulfilling their roles, had the effect of fossilising agriculture in both Libyan and Italian sectors. In Tripolitania, the British had been at great pains to keep Italian farmers on the land as a means of keeping up agricultural output, even going so far as to confirm Italian contracts originally drawn up by Italian entities. Occasional developments had taken place. The al Marj mechanised grain cultivation project was maintained by the British, while the French assisted reclamation of a small-scale irrigation project at Ghudamis. By 1951, Libyan agriculture had adjusted to low investment levels of the post-war period. In simplified terms, Tripolitania continued to have a dual economy split between Arab and Italian sectors, Cyrenaica had undergone a re-occupation by semi-nomadic groups, while Fezzan pursued its own oasis-pastoral pattern.

The arrival of political independence in 1951 had immediate and important effects on agriculture. Those lands held by the Italian state in Libya became subject to reversion to the newly independent state, including substantial areas of farmland. Italian farmers in Libya with full rights in land were faced with either coming to terms with acceptance of the new situation or repatriating themselves. Although this situation was only given clear legal form in the Italio-Libyan Accords of 1956, an Italian withdrawal from the former demographic estates became apparent from the early 1950s. In effect, with signature of the Italio-Libyan Accords, those Italian settlers in Libya wishing to retain Italian nationality had to dispose of their farms by 1962 in order to benefit from the relatively generous terms applying to repartiation of capital. Gradually to start with, but with increasing pace, the Italian farmland began to move into the hands of Libyan farmers. In Cyrenaica this implied little more than a legalisation of the *de facto* position in which former Italian estates were occupied by tribal groups with traditional claims to the territory concerned.[6] In Tripolitania the change was profound. In one region of eastern Tripolitania, lying between al Khums and Misuratah, where the author undertook fieldwork in the late 1950s, no less that 4,130 Italians left the demographic estates. By 1960 only 1,450 Italians, including dependants, were left on the estates in that area and most of these were preparing to dispose of their properties before the lapse of their benefits under the Italio-Libyan Accords.[7]

The need to facilitate transfer of lands from Italian to Libyan hands became the main task of the strategic planning of the government in the 1951-1961 period. To a significant extent the government's role was passive. Modest allocations of credits to assist farm purchases by Libyans were made, though the government was permitting up to half the value of farms as credit to Libyan applicants and by 1960 applications were coming forward at a rate of 260 a month.[8] Such activities applied almost entirely to Tripolitania since ownership of lands in Cyrenaica remained unsettled. The degree of transfer of land in Western Libya from Italian to Libyan ownership over the decade to 1961 was considerable. Even before oil exports began only 30 per cent of farmlands formerly developed as

Strategies for Agricultural Development in Libya

demographic estates was left in Italian hands.

Movement of land from Italian to Libyan farmers had a marked impact on the nature of Libyan farming. Whereas there had been little transfer of technology of irrigation technique or agronomy between the two communities before 1951, the occupation of Italian farms by Libyan owners after that date saw indigenous farmers graduating from small-scale oasis farming to medium-scale commercial farming. Libyan farmers were quick to adopt use of a different physical infrastructure on their new farms affecting irrigation, cropping patterns and housing. Libyan farming spread from the palmeries of the Tripolitanian coast out into the steppe lands in what was both economically and geographically a most radical change unequalled since by size, importance, and cost-effectiveness.

A second aspect of government strategy towards agriculture in the period 1951-61 was mobilisation of foreign aid agencies to fund and supervise development schemes in Libya. Aid from the United Kingdom and other Western European countries was channelled through the Libyan Public Development and Stabilization Agency (LPDSA) from 1952, while growing involvement of the USA was formalised in the establishment of the Libyan-American Reconstruction Commission in 1955. Criticism of the foreign aid missions that operated in Libya at this time has become fashionable.[9] Certainly, there was only slight Libyan participation in their activities. Concrete achievements in the agricultural sector were few (only Wadi Ki'am estate was completed and, despite excellent management, met with many problems). Yet, it must be conceded that the overseas aid missions were only called in by the government since it had neither the financial nor personnel resources to undertake such works on its own account. In retrospect it may be counted a blessing that the aid missions, unlike many agencies that controlled the fate of Libyan agriculture after 1961, did little or no damage to Libyan farmers or the enviroment. The creation of research, literary, cartographic and air photographic data by the agencies (including the United Nations affiliates) laid the basis on which later development could take place. A number of Libyan administrators and agricultural specialists were trained by the foreign agencies, later joining the Libyan Development Council or the Ministry of Agriculture.

While, therefore, the period between the grant of independence to Libya through the auspices of

the United Nations and the beginning of oil exports
might be characterised as one in which agriculture
experienced no more than minor development works
and a degree of stabilisation of commodity supply,
closer observation shows that real and significant
change did occur. A passive role for government
towards agricultural development proved to be
effective in the peculiar economic conditions applying at that time.

AGRICULTURE AND THE IMPACT OF OIL - 1962 TO 1969

The inflow to Libya of oil revenues after 1961,
albeit on a modest scale, induced a gradual
expansion of government intervention into the conduct of the agricultural sector. This went on
parallel to the dynamic of change within the sector
itself brought on by the re-occupation of former
Italian lands and increasing market participation
by Libyan farmers.

Despite limited access to funds, Libyan agriculture had achieved some progress before the oil
era dawned. In the first useful estimate of
national income produced by the Ministry of National
Economy in 1958 agriculture accounted for 27 per
cent of value added. In that year the sector
employed 72 per cent of the working population.
Agricultural products also fed the bulk of the Libyan
population and provided a surplus for export. That
the government felt the need to interfere in the
sector at all in a direct investment and management
sense in view of the impressive record of the
private sector is remarkable. Government control of
incoming oil revenues no doubt acted as a spur to
those in authority to assist that area of the
economy felt to be vital to the interests of the
state and all ordinary members of the rural
community. Adoption of the development plan for the
years 1963 to 1968 formalised the apparent 'need'
to involve the arms of government in agriculture.

In taking on direct responsibilities for agricultural development the government departments
failed to define their aims with any clarity. It
remains difficult to discern a particular strategy
in the plan. As late as 1966 the Ministry of
Planning and Development lacked a definitive
approach to the sector[10] and basic questions of
priorities were not resolved,[11] though it was to
the credit of that ministry that it perceived a
requirement for an appropriate strategy. In

practice, the government pursued a generally benevolent policy towards agriculture, adopting projects on an *ad hoc* basis. Specifically, the main thrust of government intervention in agriculture was through the National Agricultural Settlement Authority established under a law promulgated in July 1963 and designed to 'undertake the functions of agricultural settlement: the promotion and development of agriculture; increasing agricultural production and the improvement of the rural community ....'[12] Nasa took on the distribution of land, largely in those areas that had reverted to the Libyan state under the Italio-Libyan accord. Rather than act simply as a supervising agent, Nasa became involved in the construction, land clearance and management aspects of estate development. Its operations were entirely reminiscent of those of the former Italian organisations concerned with colonization, though in this case it was Libyans rather than aliens who were the beneficiaries. While Nasa activities were begun with the very best of intentions, its work in transferring land duplicated the already established and successful operations of the private sector. As a result, 34 per cent or £110,000,000 of the total budget for agriculture in the first five-year plan was allocated to agricultural settlement schemes under Nasa auspices merely to substitute state for private initiative in Tripolitania. The situation in Cyrenaica was more complex since there the Nasa staff were innovators.

Nasa's problems were many.[10] Shortages of staff impeded project completion. There was growing dependence on foreign consultants and companies to undertake basic construction and reclamation works. Coordination between the different branches of government concerned with rural development was rarely forthcoming.[13] Settlers on Nasa farms became increasingly reliant on the organisation for decision-making and financial support, imposing a heavy administrative and cost burden on Nasa. In Cyrenaica, where this period was mainly given over to repair of housing and land clearance on former Italian agricultural estates, Nasa appeared to have greater success than elswhere in the country, though problems over land rights and the enforcement of full-time farming remained severe.

The many difficulties facing state involvement in agriculture rarely led to official challenge of assumptions concerning the utility of such intervention. On the contrary, government strategy

became overwhelmed by the belief that the state
should be more and more concerned with the day to
day running of agriculture since, under the laisser-
faire policies before 1962, it was (wrongly) assumed
that Libyan agriculture had run down to a parlous
extent and had recovered subsequently only as a
result of government intervention.[14] Certainly,
there was need for some official action to offset
the adverse effects of Libya's expanding oil economy
on agriculture. Subsidisation of agriculture was
mooted as a means of achieving this but could only
have been a short term solution. Sadly, planning
strategy in which realities of Libya as an oil-based
economy were not brought forward. The physical
fabric of the new agriculture in Libya as created
by Nasa became no more than an extension of the
inflexible structure of demographic estates left by
the Italian colonial administration. Adoption of
rigid and hostile approaches to part-time farming,
which had previously served well as a means of
survival and a response to real economic circumstance
in Libya, became fossilized in official attitudes
to the detriment of flexibility in future planning
of the sector.

In so far as the government scored success in
the development of rural areas in the period 1962-
1969, this arose not from its agricultural strategies but from its policies towards other public
sector investment. Notably, the government gave a
geographical bias in its social and infrastructural
development programmes towards rural areas. Figures
for investment on a regional basis are not available.
It was observed during a survey of rural areas in
Libya in the period 1966-69[15] that housing, school,
hospital and public utilities programmes were
directed to the smaller settlements. The government
appeared concerned to keep the rate of rural-to-
urban migration down, possibly for political reasons.
Although losses from rural areas to the towns were
significant,[16] government spending, among other
factors, did succeed in encouraging a certain
measure of rural inertia.[17] A cost of this was
growing part-time farming. In effect, many Libyans
in rural areas diversified their sources of income
or moved from agriculture to other sectors while
remaining within their settlement of birth.

The government was not without influence on
an important trend in the private sector. Generous
credits were made available to enable the purchase
of Italian farmland. After 1961, prices of farmland
rose rapidly under the impetus of growing personal

wealth and the availability of cheap credit.
Results of the credit policies were generally not to
the advantage of either the rural community or
farming production. Credits from state agencies and
the informal sector assisted the dieselisation of
water lifting for agriculture throughout Libya,
though particularly in Tripolitania. Such
activities encouraged a rapid rise in agricultural
output, estimated at 4.5 per cent per year during
1962-67, not least through intensification of irrigation in the oases and former Italian farms together
with spread on to the extensive margin in areas such
as Ajaylat.[15] Rapid and accelerating depletion of
Libya's northern water resources was experienced as
a consequence of this investment.

    By 1969 there were deeply contradictory views
within government on the most appropriate strategy
for agricultural development. The conflicts were
amply exposed in the outline of the 1968-1973 plan.[18]
Conservation of water resources was urged yet
provision made for 'concentration on the development
of present cultivable agricultural land and the
reclamation of new lands ....' Meanwhile, Nasa
gained a reinforced role and the state took on
management of the al Kufrah production project
despite the known problems affecting the site. At a
time when the government should have been overwhelm-
ingly concerned with the continuing problems of how
best to use water in agriculture and how to adapt
the sector to economic and social change arising
from augmenting oil wealth, plans remained project-
oriented or blind to more dominant trends elsewhere
in the economy. The only saving grace in this
situation was an active private sector still
optimistic of a future in agriculture. Even here,
however, mis-placed government subsidies and
incompetence in local administration of cooperatives,
credit, extension work and marketing edged investments into wasteful areas and failed to create scope
for future advance appropriate to the realities of
an oil-dependent economy.

THE RECENT PERIOD - 1970 TO 1981

At the time of the revolution by the army officers
led by Mu'ammar al Qadhafi agriculture had importance
but was much less significant within the economy as
a whole than ten years earlier. By 1969 agriculture
contributed only 2.4 per cent of Gross Domestic

Strategies for Agricultural Development in Libya

Product and employed approximately 20 per cent of the work force. Its export value was negligible. In view of the poor agricultural base of the country and the impact of oil wealth after 1961 such a position was less bad than might have been expected.

The performance of the agricultural sector in Libya after 1969 has been well documented.[19] For the purposes of this analysis it is important to diagnose the strategies of the new government. In the immediate aftermath of the revolution political preoccupations engaged the attention of the new regime and for almost two years agricultural development became a matter of uncertainly pursuing former policies and taking on projects favoured by the ruling group. It was not until 1971/72 that a thorough review was undertaken by a set of mixed committees (Libyan and foreign) of regional priorities for agricultural development. Remarkably and despite dissenting voices on the committees, what emerged was an endorsement of the small-farm land settlement approach of the 1960s but now to be applied across a wider geographical area, including the south west and south east of the country. The model of the al Kufrah production project was also adopted in tandem with land settlement. Sarir and other sites were earmarked for new production complexes and settlement schemes in the south. It appeared, too, as if the government was prepared to substitute very large expenditures on agriculture for a realistic strategy. Allocations to agriculture rose from LD16,400,000 in 1969 to LD50,000,000 in 1970 and to LD92,800,000 in 1973 though actual disbursement probably lagged much behind these totals.

Agriculture was affected by actions of the government outside the formal budgetary and administrative framework. A decree promulgated shortly after the revolution sequestrated all Italian properties in Libya and removed permission for Italians to work on their own account. Agricultural entities involved in this move were mainly the large estates held in private and company ownership which had been un-touched by the Italo-Libyan Accord. Approximately 40,000-50,000 hectares were affected, encompassing some 450 farm units, some, such as the di Napoli farm at Tarhunah, of considerable size. In the first place the farms were put under the administration of the Institute for Land Reform and Reclamation and were later scheduled for re-allocation to Libyan farmers. In this way political expediency triumphed over economic sense. Predominantly large-scale dryland farms were to be broken up and exposed to intensification of land use under irrigation by Libyan farmers, aggravating an already serious water shortage problem. Only where citrus farms in the coastal strip were run down (as for example the Ghagur farm in Jadaydah) was the water use problem alleviated, though, in the case of several, at the price of losses of exports. At the same time, agricultural expertise was lost to Libya at the very moment that rural-to-urban migration of Libyans was coming to a new peak.

A second important step taken by the revolutionary regime was to declare that all uncultivable lands were the property of the state. This was designed above all to undermine communal land ownership, especially among the tribal groups of Cyrenaica, where in the last year of the monarchy a move had begun to settle private land titles and to permit enclosure of lands for arable cultivation. Colonel al Qadhafi was initially insistent that Libyans must work their own farms and even went as far as proclaiming that service workers in the major cities must return back to the land. The expansion of land settlement projects was, in part, a result of this belief by the Libyan leader. The concept of the Libyan as a producer with his own hands soon died, government employment expanded and foreign labour soon became a major input within the agricultural sector in Western and Southern Libya.

Private sector activities picked up fairly quickly after the revolution. Demand for foodstuffs was buoyant, credits were easily come by and the government made available subsidies on almost every item used by farmers. Land enclosure continued by individuals. Greater volumes of water were used for irrigation. A number of enterprising farmers took on animal raising and poultry farming. Expansion of the urban areas and the conversion of agricultural lands to residential or amenity use went on unabated. The policies outlined in the Green Book, which so crushingly affected housing and industry, were extremely mild in respect of agriculture. But by the late 1970s the spreading government intrusion on all private sector enterprise began to have adverse effects on farmers. Arbitrary actions or administrative incompetence disrupted farm supplies, all imported sources of which were state controlled. Growing fears that the government would enforce full-time farming and, in the coastal strip of Western Libya, threats of major land re-distribution brought deepening insecurity to the farming community. On the basis of a number of case studies of private farms in Western Libya, undertaken by the author, investment fell off sharply in the late 1970s. Only housing for owner occupance seemed to survive as a significant area of activity.

In retrospect, the 1970s may be assessed as a period in which there was never an overall strategy for agriculture. Belief in high spending in the sector together with adoption of large scale irrigation projects in themselves precluded integrated planning of agriculture. It was impossible to square dramatic and expensive experiments with the realities of labour shortages or the need for creation of a future economically viable productive base at the end of the oil era, in spite of the optimism of outside observers.[20]

Only in one dimension were discernible government policies achieved. The state did become the paramount force within agriculture over the period. Its intervention was to be seen almost everywhere though the private sector was far from being overthrown and total socialisation of agriculture had not yet been achieved.

STRATEGIES FOR THE FUTURE

During the closing years of the 1970s the government began the task of planning for the period to the end of the century (1981-2000). Few Libyans with an educated interest in social and economic planning would deny that these twenty years will be critical ones for Libya. Unless there are substantial new finds of oil beneath the soil or off-shore, the country will be coming towards the end of or have already exhausted its potential for significant crude oil exports. Declining reserves and rising domestic consumption will force the country to find alternative sources than oil for generating foreign exchange earnings and treasury revenues. The production to reserves ratio at the end of 1980 stood at more than 1:30 but in view of very large use of fuel inside Libya official forecasts suggest that exports will be reduced rapidly and cease before the end of the century.

The implications for agriculture of a gradual diminution of crude oil exports and the end of the rentier economy[21] are considerable. Once again the sector will be looked to for provision of domestic food supply, some exports and as a major source of employment. In the past, when standards of living were lower and aspirations less than they presently are, ingenious plans were elaborated for maximum use of agriculture for generating employment and income.[2] Agriculture had, by 1980, lost its potential in both these roles. This arose not simply because of changed attitudes towards agricultural employment by the Libyan population but because there were real alterations in the physical resource base between the 1950s and the 1980s. The boom in agriculture that affected the 1960s and 1970s systematically exploited limited and fast declining water reserves in the northern areas of the country.[19] Expert opinion indicated that radical reduction in water use in the Gefara was vital if permanent damage was not to be sustained.[22] In effect, Libya's richest agricultural area and one of sophisticated and productive agriculture was at risk of losing its irrigation potential. Government plans for the Gefara coastal strip under discussion in 1980 and 1981 included a land redistribution programme, enforcement of full-time farming, a managed crop rotation, and greater state control of day-to-day farming activities. All this was designed to reduce water use in agriculture by two thirds. The strategy options open to the government in this vital area were increasingly constrained by environmental-physical limitations, its own past policies of misplaced subsidies, and inflexibilities derived from an inappropriate agrarian structure inherited from the Italian administration but extended in the year after 1963.

It was also clear by 1980 that the large-scale irrigation developments on the al Kufrah model in the south of the country were running into severe difficulties. While the Perspective Plan made the assumption that a major degree of land settlement should take place in the Libyan south, including sites such as Sarir and al Kufrah, it was apparent that intensive demographic settlement was facing great difficulties. Migration of Libyan workers and staff to the new production and land settlement projects in the decade 1970-80 had been negligible. Indeed, the projects had made no appreciable impact on out-migration from the south of the indigenous peoples. Costs of the agricultural development projects in the south appeared to have a capital cost at least eight times that of farms established in the coastal areas.[4] High overhead costs arose from longhaul transport and extreme climatic conditions at the sites. It is difficult to argue with the view that both settlement and production farms in the south would survive only for as long as the government was able to make available subsidies and that, once oil wealth began to fail, the farms would be economically unviable even taking the charitable view that farmers could be found to settle and would remain long-term in the south.

Loss of the Gefara as an area of expansion and intensification together with exposure of the frailty and high cost of the southern agricultural projects changed very considerably the openings for future development of agriculture in Libya. There was deep uncertainty on the best way forward and in 1981 a special committe of Libyan experts was set up to review the findings of the draft regional plans 1981-2000 for the four planning areas - Benghazi, Tripoli, al Khalij and Sabhah. Doubtless this committee will formulate sensible and balanced policies for agriculture within a framework of the economy as a whole and will particularly take account of Libya's deteriorating oil export position as it moves towards the end of the century. In the past, political considerations have always supervened to upset or eclipse the development programmes formulated by the economic and social planners. Such an eventuality is likely again during the 1980s despite the realities of declining strength in oil reserves and the failures in Gefaran and southern agricultures unless the government can, albeit belatedly, accept that high spending on isolated projects does not constitute a strategy for so important an area of the economy. Equally, cognizance that all agricultural activities should offer the prospect of ultimate economic viability and therefore survival after oil exports on a large scale cease is necessary among the political decision-makers. Without such appreciable changes in official approaches to agriculture strategies for agricultural development in Libya will be incomplete and possibly irrelevant to the country's real future needs.

Notes

1. Allan, J.A., McLachlan, K.S., and Penrose E.T., 1971, *Libya: agriculture and economic development*, Cass, London
2. Rowland, F. and Robb, E., 1945, *Survey of land resources in Tripolitania*, British Military Administration, Tripoli
3. Joffe, G.H., 1981, 'Social and political

structures in the Gefara Plain in the late nineteenth century' paper delivered to conference on Economic and Social Development of Libya in the Late Nineteenth and Twentieth Centuries, SOAS, London University

4. Speerplan GmbH and Finnmap Oy, 1980, *Al Khalij region - draft report of the regional plan 1981-2000*, Secretariat of Municipalities, Tripoli, See especially Chapters 1-5, 7 and 10

5. Moore, M., 1940, *Fourth Shore, Italy's mass colonisation of Libya*, Routledge, London

6. Buru, M.M., 1960, *A geographical study of the Eastern Jebel Akhdar, Cyrenaica*, unpublished thesis, Durham University

7. McLachlan, K.S., 1961, *A geographical study of the coastal zone between Homs and Misurata*, unpublished thesis in four volumes, Durham University, p 666

8. Fowler, G.L., 1973, 'Decolonization of rural Libya' in *Annals of the Association of American Geographers*, Volume 63, No 4, December 1974, p 524

9. First, R., 1974, *Libya: the elusive revolution*, Penguin, Hardmondworth, p 142

10. Lalevic, D.L. and Lalevic, M., 1965, *Implementation of agricultural settlement*, Ministry of Planning and Development, Tripoli

11. Farley, R., 1965, *Commentary No 11, a note on a report by Lalevic, Schmeyla and Lalevic, Agriculture in Libya and plan for its development*, Ministry of Planning and Development, Tripoli

12. Government of Libya, 1963, *Law concerning the National Agricultural Settlement Authority*, 27th Sarar 1963, Benghazi

13. Lalevic, D.L., Schmeyla, M.A., and Lalevic, M., 1966, *List of principal recommendations for agricultural development in Libya*, Ministry of Planning and Development, Tripoli. Also see *Status of Libyan Agriculture and main lines for its development*, Ministry of Planning and Development, Tripoli

14. Attiga, A.A., 1971, 'The economic impact of oil on Libyan agriculture' in Allan et al 1971, *op cit* p 11

15. Allan, J.A., McLachlan, K.S., 1971, 'Land use and cropping patterns: present position and recent change' in Allan et al 1971, *op cit* pp 100-103

16. Hartley, R.G., 1972, 'Libya: economic development and demographic responses' in Clarke, J.I., and Fisher, W.B., *Population of the Middle East and North Africa*, London University Press, London, p 325

17. Libyan-London Universities Joint Research

Project, 1969, *Libya*, Volume 3, London p 100

18. Kingdom of Libya, 1968, *Objectives of the second five year plan 1968-1973*, National Planning Council, Tripoli, p14

19. Allan, J.A., 1981, *Libya:the experience of oil*, Croom Helm/Westview, London/Boulder

20. George, A.R., 1973, 'Kufrah: the desert's hidden resources' in *Middle East International*, No 25, London, pp 15-18

21. Mabro, R., 1969, 'La Libye, Un etat rentier?' in Project No 39, November 1969, pp 1090-1101

22. Bakhbakhi, A., 1981, Private communication in which it was warned that the salt water/fresh water interface in the Gefara would soon penetrate on an irregular front as far inland as Bin Gashir, more than 20 kilometres from the coast

Chapter 3
CAPITAL HAS NOT SUBSTITUTED FOR WATER IN AGRICULTURE

J.A.Allan

INTRODUCTION

The responsibility for setting agricultural policy in the twentieth century fell to governments with widely different political goals. All, however, had high expectations of the country's agricultural resources. The record of agricultural development in Libya is one of continual readjustment of the agricultural goals of increased production and productivity to the realities of the limiting resource, water. Libya's renewable groundwater resources are modest and her fossil water though considerable is limited.

After a brief review of the history of water-resource use in the twentieth century the chapter deals with the 1970s, which was a particularly interesting decade because it was in this period that the potential of the country's water resources was most extensively and comprehensively tested. In the 1970s an attempt was made to combine a substantial proportion (20 per cent approximately) of the oil derived development budget with the soil and water resources of rural Libya. The experience of the 1970s has demonstrated the need for an agricultural development policy which subordinates economic, political and social considerations to the optimum management of water (and the technology which facilitates such management). Though capital has not yet been found to be readily substitutable for water, there is still considerable scope for a more effective combination of these factors, and some of the technological and institutional options will be discussed.

Capital has not Substituted for Water in Agriculture

LIBYA'S WATER RESOURCES

Libya's current and medium-term prosperity depends on its oil resources and their continued sale at prices consistent with world inflation. Sustained prosperity on the other hand will only be achieved when the agricultural and industrial sectors develop self-generated, unsubsidised and 'economic' systems of production. In this discussion only the position of the *agricultural sector* will be evaluated, and special emphasis will be given to those resources which set limits to investment and development options. Water is the unavoidable and the most difficult of the constraints, but institutional deficiencies have also proved to be limiting and capital should not be viewed as limitless, even in oil-enriched Libya, and an 'opportunity cost' approach to the use of investment resources is relevant. The discussion will also deal with the perceptions of Libya's administrators, leaders and farmers of their country's resources, since it is according to these perceptions that decisions on the use of water have been made. The decisions of the past two decades at national and individual farmer level have clearly implied that water resources were *not considered to be limited*, and further that the investment of capital to raise and distribute water would create a productive combination of those 'factors' whose combination normally leads to viable and even profitable agricultural enterprises.

Figure 1 summarises a study by Pallas[1] of Libya's water use in the mid-1970s and the anticipated use by the end of the century. He noted that 97 per cent of the water was drawn from the ground in the mid-1970s. Libya has no flowing water and rainfall is significant only in small coastal tracts of the Gefara Plain and the Jabal Nafusah in the north-west and in the Jabal al Akhdar in the north-east. Rainfed farming is limited to the Gefara, and to the coastal and adjacent uplands, an area in all totalling about 100,000 square kilometres.

Libya's groundwater falls into two categories. First there are renewable resources in the coastal plains of Tripoli, Benghazi and near Misuratah, and secondly in the south there are substantial fossil water resources which have been dated to be between 6,000 and 30,000 years old.[2] The quantification of Libya's groundwater is subject to widely different interpretation, but the Pallas figures on water use are likely to be within 30 per cent of an as yet

Capital has not Substituted for Water in Agriculture

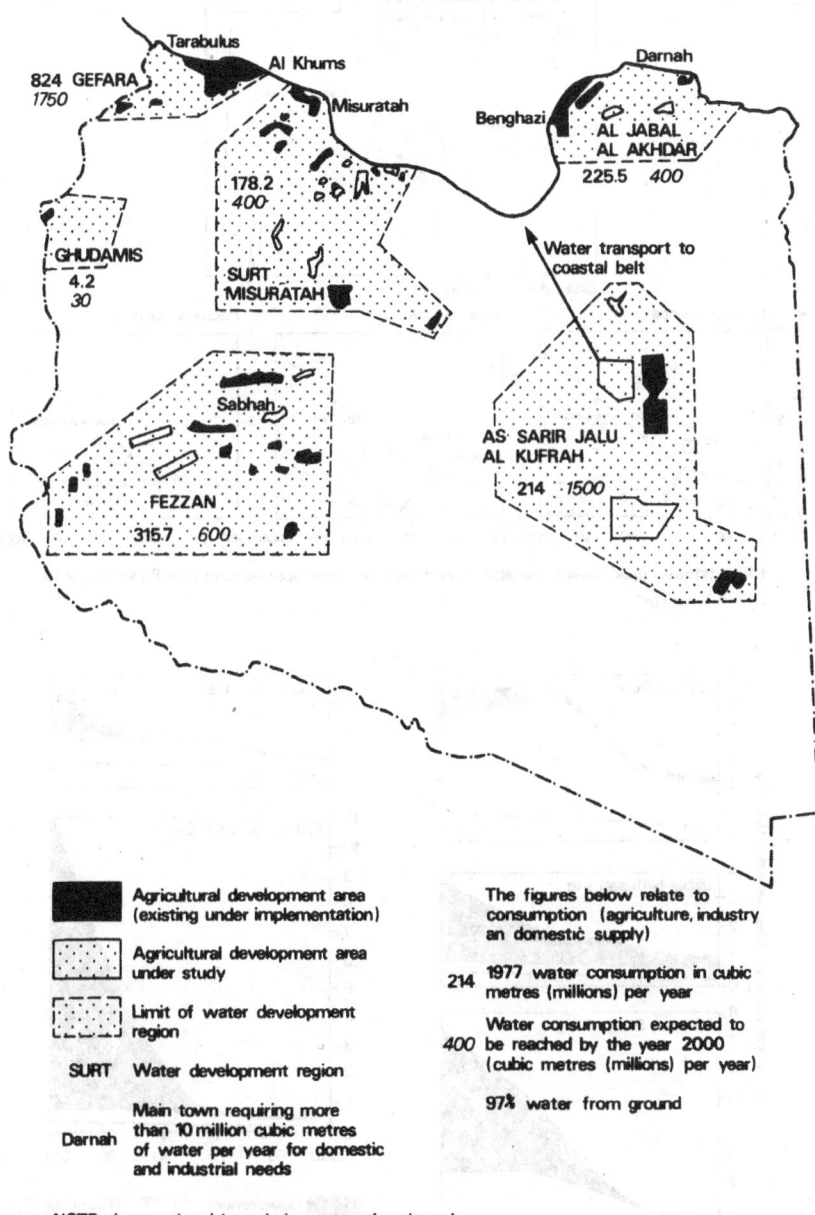

Figure 2 Water Development Regions and Agricultural Development Areas
Source: Pallas P [1]

Capital has not Substituted for Water in Agriculture

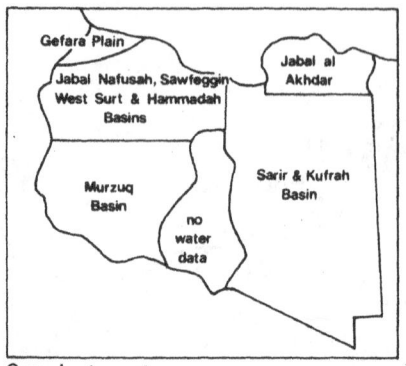

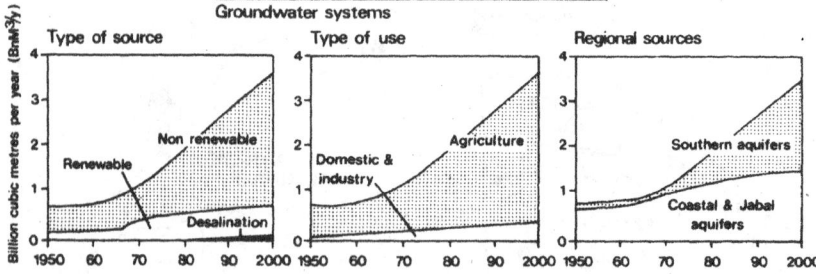

The estimates upon which the above are based are very approximate and Pallas suggests a ±30% margin.

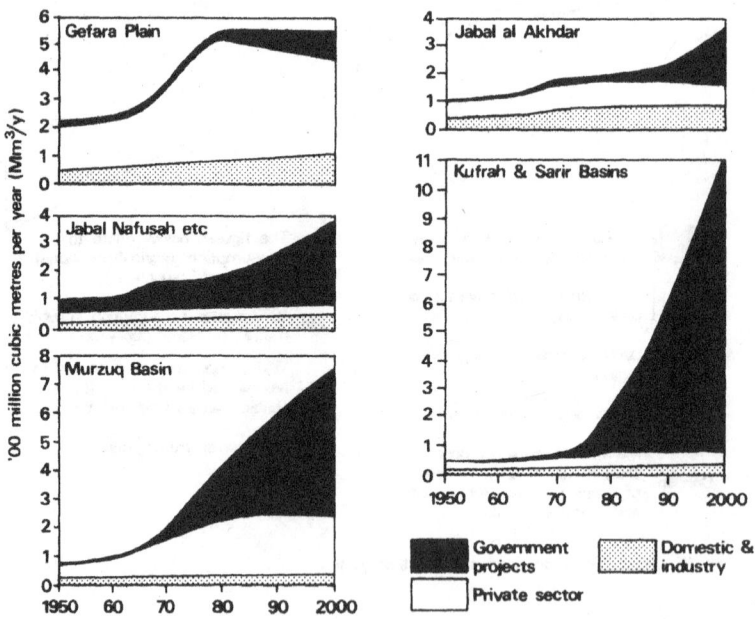

Figure 3 Water Resource Development 1950-2000 by Region and Type of Use   Source: Pallas P[1]

unresearchably accurate figure.

The renewable water has been used so heavily, and especially since 1965, that in the Gefara the rate of use was estimated to be six times the rate of recharge in 1981.[3] Soon the coastal resource will not be available for agricultural, industrial or urban use, especially as it will have been damaged, possibly irreperably by sea-water intrusion. The fossil water in the south has scarcely been touched and it is this resource which will provide water for all users in the years to the end of the century. The south will see further *in situ* development but will also provide water for enterprises at the coast. It is difficult to give reliable figures for the levels at which water extraction could be sustained but it seems likely that the south will be able to yield water at the rate of two billion cubic metres per year for up to fifty years (compare the annual flow of the Nile at Aswan of approximately 60 billion cubic metres, and Egypt's annual agricultural water use of close to 40 billion cubic metres). Libya's water resources are, therefore, by no means negligible, but by their nature they are limited. Renewable water has been mismanaged almost out of existence, and the remaining resources have to be approached in a particularly careful manner, so that returns to the precious water, are maximised.

CHANGING PERCEPTIONS OF WATER RESOURCES AND POLICY CONSEQUENCES.

Renewable natural resources such as soil and water are particularly vulnerable to damage by modern technology and especially when such technologies are deployed by agencies and individuals with misconceptions about the robustness or volume of the resource being managed. Traditional technologies for groundwater use are generally 'soft' on the resource as their capacities to raise water are limited. One traditional Libyan well might have irrigated one hectare intensively when the water lay less than ten metres down reflecting an annual water utilisation of 10,000 cubic metres, which would irrigate one hectare for a year. In these circumstances small farms or partially irrigated farms were the rule in coastal Libya. Mechanised pumps first became available in the 1920s and 1930s, but it was not until the early 1960s that their adoption took off at a rate which has proved to be universally damaging to the coastal aquifers.

Perceptions of Libya's renewable resources have varied in relation to the length of the experience gained in managing them. Thus the Italian enthusiasm concerning the agricultural potential of Libya's renewable resources was tempered by the reality of handling them.[4] The limited extent of the coastal aquifers was quickly established by the Italian geologists.[5] The shallow aquifers were limited in development potential - the deep aquifers were generally saline. As a result Italian water management policies included controls which specified the spacing and capacity of wells and additionally the rates of water extraction. Nevertheless groundwater levels did decline in areas to the south of Tripoli. For example at Suwani bin Yadim water had fallen over ten metres by 1940. Similar patterns of water use prevailed during the years up to independence in 1951.

Independent Libya was extremely poor and after the model suggested by Fanon[6] gained its independence in 1951, 'in exchange for the maintenance of an economic dependency'. This dependency conditioned the aid-orientated economy and only limited resources were available for agricultural investment including the development of irrigated farming. The 1950s, witnessed some very successful private sector irrigated farming, which paradoxically demonstrated the potential of the coastal water resources for citrus farming without signifying the problems implicit in the high water use systems. The paradox lay in the apparent success of the 'inappropriate' systems, for they were emulated enthusiastically in the middle-1960s and afterwards with oil-revenue derived investment, by individual farmers in the private sector.

The contrary advice of Libyan and consultant hydrogeologists was eventually heard by members of the pre-revolutionary Libyan government, and the awareness of the limited absorptive capacity of the agricultural sector for capital investment was publicly embraced in the five year plan overtaken by the 1969 revolution. A lower proportion of the development budget was wisely allocated to agriculture than in earlier plans.[7] A decade of handling investment in a marginal environment had conditioned Libya's, by then small group of technocrats, to approach the combination of capital and water with caution.

Capital has not Substituted for Water in Agriculture

The expensively won wisdom of the 1960s was relearned at enormous expense in the 1970s. The new leadership which guided investment after 1969 proceeded on the assumption that the country could be made green. 'The Agricultural Revolution is now continuing in the fields where it will progress day after day, multiplying its revenues year after year and, with God's assistance, it will transform our land left for too long neglected and desert, into richly fertile soil, which shall abundantly reward our struggling people, who liberated it from all colonialist intruders'.[8] The book in which this quotation appeared also included the following dedication:

> In the name of God Most Gracious, Most Merciful. It is He who sends down rain from the sky: from it ye drink, and out of it (grows) the vegetation on which ye feed your cattle. With it He produces for you corn, olives, date-palms, grapes and every kind of fruit: verily in this is a Sign for those who give thought.[9]

The thesis of the Libyan leader would seem to be that Libya's resources have long been ripe for development and it was political impediments which alone denied to Libya the effective development of its 'richly fertile soil'. This unfortunate starting point has led to an extraordinarily extravagant and ineffective agricultural record in the 1970s, and expecially with respect to the use of water with which we are concerned here.

Ignoring the signs that the private sector irrigated farms on the Gefara Plain was gaining increased levels of agricultural production at the expense of the region's long term agricultural viability, the revolutionary regime continued to support, subsidise and extend irrigated farming. By 1976 awareness of the dilemma was registered when discouragement of citrus planting followed another would-be conservaţionist measure, the closing of the tomato paste factories. Both citrus and tomatoes utilise large volumes of water; citrus for example requires upwards of one metre depth of water per year when watered by sprinkler-irrigation systems. Unfortunately because there were no effective means to monitor the extent of the irrigated area, never mind the volume of water used by the individual farmer, the exhortations to reduce water use went unheeded. Water use increased and

Capital has not Substituted for Water in Agriculture

the dramatic declines in groundwater levels described in the following section occurred.

A decade on from the revolution the wisdom of Libyan hydrogeologists and consultants was finally adopted by the Libyan leadership, and water conservation policies were claimed to be part of an ambitious scheme to reorganise farming in the coastal area, although first impressions of the endeavour suggest that far too much attention is being given to the relatively unimportant matter of arranging the equitable distribution of land, when the optimisation of the use of water is the urgent and clear priority. In relation to water there is no shortage of land in Libya, and land tenure policy should be concerned mainly to maximise the effective combination of technology and water, on the very small tracts which Libya's limited water resources will irrigate. The title of the chapter suggests that the experience to date has been of an unsuccessful combination of water and capital. Investment in irrigation has substantially increased production since 1960, but the style of the investment has not been consistent with a sustained use of the water resources. The technologies deployed have made larger volumes of water available than was possible by traditional methods, and to some extent there has been an appropriate sustitution of capital for labour, of which Libya is also short. But to date the investment has *not* been directed to substituting for water in the sense of introducing irrigation systems which will allow one cubic metre of water to support two or even three times the area of crops currently supported. Such technologies are expensive but in Libya there is really no dilemma; *water* is the limiting resource. *Capital* has until recently been relatively unconstrained. An approach which ensures a high return to each cubic metre of water should be pursued, and returns to the other factors, land, capital and labour, could, and probably should, be less critically evaluated.

WATER USE AND ITS IMPACT ON THE RESOURCE

The history of agricultural policy and of water use have been reflected in the fall in the groundwater levels of the coastal aquifers. The safe yield of an aquifer is equivalent to the average annual recharge. The recharge is in turn directly related to the annual precipitation of the catchment. It has taken many years to arrive at a figure for the

Capital has not Substituted for Water in Agriculture

Gefara Plain system, but by 1980 it was generally agreed that the safe yield of the system was 100 million cubic metres. By 1940 this safe yield had probably begun to be exceeded as a progressive decline in groundwater levels was evident.[9] The trend in water extraction continued at the same rate until the early 1960s when additional pumping began on the private sector holdings created as the result of the sale and subdivision of large Italian farms. Observation well records of the Soil and Water Conservation Department of the Ministry of Agriculture clearly demonstrated the trend by 1968[10] and a one metre per year rate of decline at points 40 kilometres from the coast was obviously going to become a three metres per year annual decline in a few years time. In the event the three metres/year rate occurred by 1973 and five metres/year was being recorded by 1980. These data and other indirect measures of water use suggest that the rate of withdrawal in the Gefara system was running at 600 million cubic metres/year, or about six times the rate of recharge.

The impact in the groundwater resource had been severe. By 1981 the water at points such as Bin Gashir and Suwani bin Yadim had been pumped to below sea level so that the gradient in the aquifer ran south away from the sea. The problem of sea-water intrusion had already affected coastal farms, and by 1980 it affected the wells six kilometres inland which supplied Tripoli city.

Figure 2 indicates for both the coastal aquifers and the southern fossil groundwater Pallas'[1] estimates of water use in the recent past and up to the year 2000. The diagramms point up the problems with the coastal resources, and emphasise the demands that are likely to be placed on Libya's finite southern water resources.

AN AGRICULTURAL DEVELOPMENT POLICY CONSISTENT WITH
THE LIMITING RESOURCE

The agricultural options available to Libya have been shown to be extremely restricted. The direction taken in the Gefara area in the 1960s had been proved both uneconomic and unsustainable by 1969, and by the end of the 1970s had led to the serious consequence of the possible irreversible pollution of the resource by sea-water intrusion. An agricultural strategy must therefore be devised which is low in water use and which maximises the effectiveness

Capital has not Substituted for Water in Agriculture

of each cubic metre pumped.

In the Gefara it would seem to be necessary to reduce the irrigated area from the 1980 figure of 90-100,000 hectares[11] irrigated or partially irrigated to only 20,000 hectares and these 20,000 hectares should only be irrigated by water efficient systems such as trickle irrigation, which can reduce water use from over one metre depth per year to only 300mm per year for such crops as citrus.[12] Even with this drastic reduction no provision has been made for urban and industrial use. Desalinised water could make a significant contribution to these last uses, but even so a sustainable withdrawal will be difficult by the end of the century. It could even be argued that all irrigated farming should cease on the Gefara Plain.

In these circumstances the importance of the fossil water in the south is crucial, and its long term significance is even greater than its current value. Certainly there is a need to experiment to determine economical methods of raising crops in the south and elsewhere but at a time when food is relatively cheap in the world market there is no point in using irreplaceable water on extravagent and risky agricultural ventures in the remote south. The opportunity cost of wasting water in the 1980s should be valued in terms of the agricultural production which will be foregone in the future when world food prices will have inflated to such an extent that indigenous food production will make economic, as well as strategic, sense. Plans are well advanced at the time of writing to bring up to two billion cubic metres of water from Tazerbo and Sarir to the coast in the east of the country, and up to one billion cubic metres from the Fezzen to alleviate the water deficiencies on the Gefara Plain. If oil revenues flow satisfactorily these ventures could be financed, but it behoves those planning these ambitious water transportation schemes to ensure that the agricultural systems which would be fed by them have been evaluated on the basis of returns to water outlined here. All agricultural ventures must be evaluated in terms of their returns to water, and the evaluation of returns to land, labour and capital must be subordinated to the evaluation of water efficiency. That capital has not substituted satisfactorily for water in the first two decades of oil revenues should not be taken as a final statement. Capital remains a prerequisite for the deployment of the expensive trickle and glass-house technologies which are the only

Capital has not substituted for Water in Agriculture

viable irrigation options for Libya.

Notes

1. Pallas, P., 1978, *Water resources in the Socialist People's Libyan Arab Jamahiriya*, Secretariat of Dams and Water Resources, Tripoli, pp 88
2. Wright, E.P., 1977, 'Groundwater resources in Eastern Libya' in *Report of the Society for Libyan Studies*, Vol 8, pp 41-44
3. Latham, J.S., et al., 1981, *Monitoring the changing areal extent of irrigated lands of the Gefara Plain, Libya*, Secretariat of Agricultural Reclamation and Land Development, Tripoli
4. Wright, J., 1981, 'Libya Italy's promised land' paper presented at the conference on Economic and social development of Libya in the late nineteenth and twentieth centuries
5. Desio, A., 1940, 'Sulla posizione geologica e sullorigine delle falde aquifere artesiano Gefara', *l° di Geologia di Milano*, Publication No 13, Milan
6. Fanon, F., 1964, *Toward the African revolution*, English translation published 1967 and available in 1980 by Readers and Writers Publishing, London pp 197. See page 125
7. Allan, J.A., 1981, *Libya: the experience of oil*, Croom Helm, London, pp 340
8. Qadhafi, M., 1978, Speech by Colonel Qadhafi quoted in Jabel al Akhdar Authority, *Harvest in all seasons in the Jabal al Akhdar*, Benghazi, pp 127
9. Cederstrom, C.J., and Bertaiola, M., 1960, *Groundwater resources of the Tripoli area Libya*, USOM Report, Tripoli
10. Allan, J.A., McLachlan, K.S., and Penrose, E.T., 1973, *Libya: agriculture and economic development*, Cass, London, pp 214
11. FAO, 1981, Estimates by Gefara Plain water utilisation study, for Secretariat of Agriculture, Tripoli
12. Chanduri, F., and Kullab, I., 1980, *Drip irrigation in citrus as compared to traditional irrigation methods in the Tripoli area*, Soil and Irrigation Research Unit, Secretariat of Agricultural Reclamation and Land Development, Tripoli, pp 32. See page 18

Development of the Libyan Oil Industry

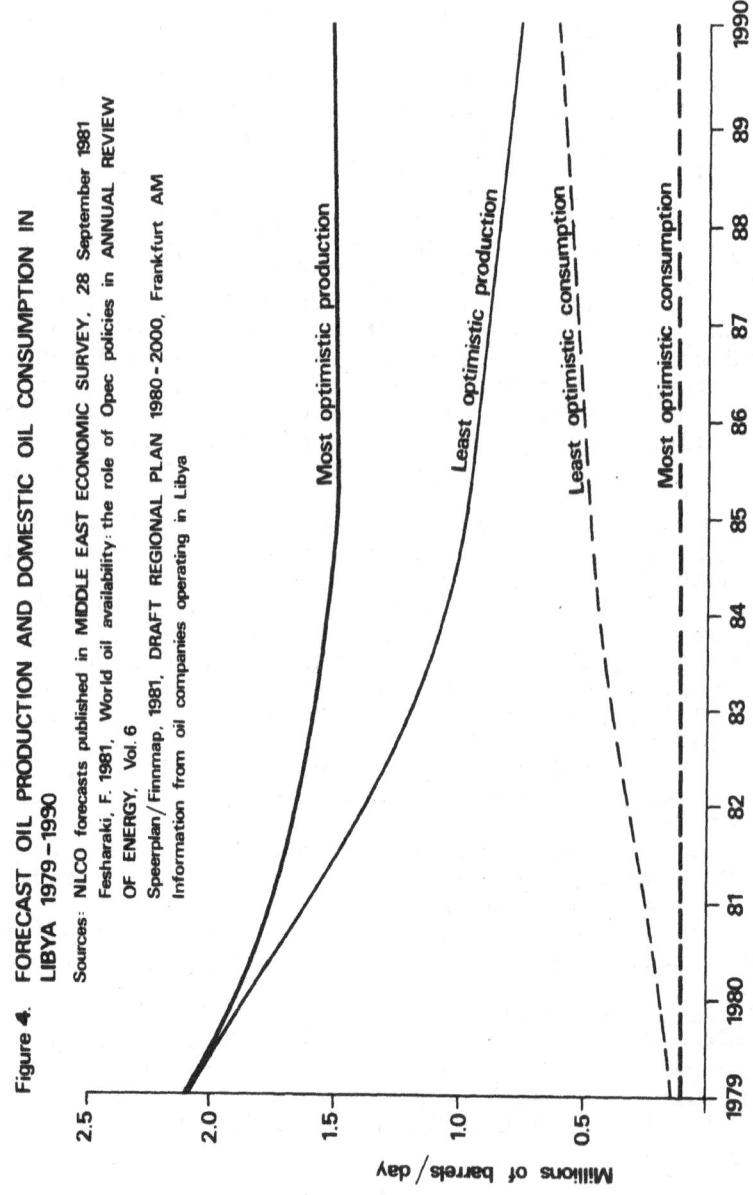

Figure 4. FORECAST OIL PRODUCTION AND DOMESTIC OIL CONSUMPTION IN LIBYA 1979-1990

Sources: NLCO forecasts published in MIDDLE EAST ECONOMIC SURVEY, 28 September 1981
Fesharaki, F. 1981, World oil availability: the role of Opec policies in ANNUAL REVIEW OF ENERGY, Vol. 6
Speerplan/Finnmap, 1981, DRAFT REGIONAL PLAN 1980-2000, Frankfurt AM
Information from oil companies operating in Libya

Chapter 4
DEVELOPMENT OF THE LIBYAN OIL INDUSTRY

P.Barker & K.S.McLachlan

"To build oil refineries for when the oil runs out smacks of black humour rather than development policy" Paul Stevens, 'Saudi Arabia's oil policy in the 1970s' in Niblock (ed) *State, society and economy in Saudi Arabia*, Croom Helm, London, 1982.

INTRODUCTION

This chapter examines the contemporary Libyan oil and natural gas industry against which developments elsewhere in the Libyan economy can be seen in the special context of oil dependence. Acknowledgement is made of the authors' debt to those detailed analyses of the Libyan oil industry published by Ghanem (1975)[1] and Waddhams (1980)[2] which have been freely drawn on in this chapter. Latest production and export statistics are, however, included together with a report on the progress of the renewed exploration effort. In the second part of the chapter forecast patterns of production, domestic oil consumption, and the rate of depletion of reserves are examined. Using objective criteria it is shown that Libya, under the worst of circumstances, could become a net importer of crude oil by the mid-1990s, an estimate that undermines the conventional assessment that reserves could sustain exports through past the end of the century.[3]

THE CONTEMPORARY HYDROCARBONS INDUSTRY IN LIBYA

First traces of Libya's oil wealth were recorded as early as 1914[4] but it was not until independence and the passage of the Minerals Law of 1953 that international oil companies were invited to begin preliminary geological reconnaissance. The situation changed quickly with the passing of the first Petroleum Law in April 1955[5] under the terms of which oil concessions were allocated. The Suez crisis of 1956 did much to enhance Libya's position in the eyes of the oil companies which became more eager to find sources of oil west of the Suez Canal. By 1960 there were twenty oil companies exploring in Libyan territory in 95 concession areas that took in some 65 per cent of the land surface of the country.[6] Libya became an oil-exporter from 1961. Thereafter oil production and exports rose rapidly, the terminals handling 14,400 barrels/day (b/d) in 1961 and 3,312,900 b/d by 1969[7] as the government followed a volume oriented oil policy. So accelerated a rate of growth was brought about by the country's considerable real needs as the state sought to mitigate the extreme deprivation generally experienced until that time (UN estimates suggested a per capita income before oil exploitation of approximately $75 per annum). The international companies were in most cases eager to encourage an expansion of Libyan oil exports for their own ends, while Libya lacked the trained cadres capable of comprehending the international oil market and the means of controlling the oil companies.

As early as 1957 the Libyan government felt doubts concerning the terms given to concessionaires under the 1955 Petroleum Law and had begun to tighten up specific articles of the individual concession agreements. By 1961 serious amendment was required since the original law was imprecise on the matter of pricing of oil exports. The law neither obliged oil companies to publish prices for Libyan crudes nor mentioned the term "posted price". An amended law was promulgated in July 1961 together with Petroleum Regulation No 6[8], which detailed the procedures for posting prices. In August 1961 Esso posted a price of $2.21 per barrel of $39°$ API gravity oil. The Libyan authorities were ill-disposed to the price set by Esso and claimed that the company had failed to satisfy the conditions of the new petroleum law[9], which required agreement between company and government before posting. Esso had also, claimed official spokesmen, failed to take account of the high gravity[10] and low sulphur content of Libyan crude oil in posting a price. Protests against the Esso posted price were of no avail.

Protection for Libya against the unilateral actions of the oil companies only came later through the formation of Opec in 1960 after which the inter-

Development of the Libyan Oil Industry

national oil companies were discouraged or prevented from lowering posted prices. Libya joined Opec in 1962 and benefited from the Opec royalty expensing agreement of 1965[11], which was incorporated in a further amendment of the Petroleum Law.[12]

In 1968 all concession holders were issued with copies of Petroleum Regulation No 8[13], which comprised the pro-forma, 47-article, Conservation Regulation adopted at the November 1968 Baghdad Opec meeting.[14] This regulation effectively transferred to government control all company operations affecting oilfield practices. Strictly speaking it was not a legal regulation as it was never published in the Official Gazette, nor was it binding on holders of existing concessions since changes in agreements had to be mutually acceptable. In the event, the regulation became vitally important during the period immediately following the Revolution of 1969 as the government was able to use it to force the oil companies to reduce production as part of the strategy designed to make them accept higher prices for crude oil. Companies operating in Libya eventually complied with the regulation under the terms of the Tripoli Agreement of 1971.[15]

Initially, the Revolution of 1969 did not affect oil operations in Libya. But in May 1970 a series of cuts[16] in allowable production levels was introduced to force up posted prices. The new government's tough stance against the oil companies was instrumental in breaking the pattern of stable posted prices that had held since 1960. Price rises[17] caused by the conflict of the Libyan government with the oil companies greatly facilitated the 1971 Tehran Agreement[18] between Opec and the oil majors and it was in this brief period that Libya enjoyed its greatest influence within Opec, bolstered by its large share of total Opec crude oil output (comprising 15 per cent in 1970)[19] and support from other Opec members for which Libya's shift to a radical price oriented policy was advantageous. Subsequently Libya lost its leading role within Opec as it was outmanoeuvred by other producers.

Libyan interests persisted in calling for higher prices throughout the 1970s. In the absence of Opec production programming, however, it had to rely on market crises to achieve real increases[20] in unit prices. At times the Libyan position was counterproductive, leading to low and economically damaging levels of lifting by the international oil companies. Nationalisation of oil company operations in Libya in 1973[21] reflected the moderating influence of Opec on participation agreements although relations between the Libyan government and the oil companies were far from good in that period and exploration activities suffered[22] in consequence. In 1974, following the part-nationalisations, the Libyan authorities signed a number of product-sharing joint ventures[23], which, if successful, could have offered attractive returns to those foreign companies involved. A further round was initiated in 1980 in the hope of stimulating more exploration in the country.

Libyan policies towards oil production were not characterised by the same consistency as its desire to see a higher unit price paid for its oil. A first reduction in output in the period 1970-71 was mainly a measure to force the hands of the oil companies on price increases. There is some evidence that the Libyan government would like to reclaim a position of importance within Opec through higher production and in 1978, when preparations for the 1981-2000 national perspective[3] plan was being drawn up, it was assumed that oil production would rise to some 3.6 million b/d during the course of the 1980s. In 1979, as prices rose, so the Libyan authorities brought their production ceiling down to 2.5 million b/d , although actual output averaged less than this. During 1980 the production was again lowered to 1.75 million b/d[24]. Conservation had now become a major concern for Libya and could no longer be considered as a mere pricing gambit. The Minister for Oil, Abdessalam Zagaar, announced that production from existing fields was scheduled to fall to some 1.3 to 1.4 million b/d by 1985[25]. In the long term, the constraining element on policies towards oil production was seen as "Whatever the rate of production adopted, it is essential that reserves should be held to support the new petrochemical industries for a long period ahead".[26]

The Libyan government evolved no clearly defined policy on natural gas, despite extensive plans for gas-based industrialisation. Utilization of associated gas was generally encouraged by Petroleum Regulation Number 8 governing conservation, which imposed penalties for excessive flaring of gas. With the exception of two fields formerly owned by Esso[27], all other natural gas fields were abandoned with their wells plugged. Libya carried its hard negotiating position on oil prices into the area of liquified natural gas exports but with only limited success.

Development of the Libyan Oil Industry

HYDROCARBON RESOURCES

The greatest concentrations of hydrocarbons in Libya were located in the al Khalij region, largely within the Surt Basin, which comprised a structure of Mesozoic-Tertiary origins including strata of marine clastic and carbonate sediments[28]. Hydrocarbons appear in basement Lower Palaeozoic horst blocks overlain by Mesozoic or Tertiary sediments. The oil reservoirs were for the most part small in comparison to those found on the southern side of the Gulf and occurred in the carbonates, being capped with shales. Towards the south eastern extension of the Surt Basin, oil and natural gas were found in Cretaceous sandstones, notably at Sarir.

Libya's second oil-bearing area was in the west of the country. Western districts were favoured for exploration during the 1950s since commercial discoveries of oil had been made in Algeria at Edjele, close to the Libyan border. Esso Standard Libya took up the first Libyan concession in November 1955 in Concession 1[6] in the south west and found oil, though not in commercial quantities. Gulf Oil of Libya located significant oil further east in Zone 1[29] and, together with other exploration activities in adjacent concessions, some 80,000-100,000 b/d was estimated to be available in the western area. Development of the western oilfields was delayed by disputes between the Libyan Government and the oil companies, the latter contending that commercial operation of the deposits was not feasible[29]. A pipeline serving the west was begun in 1977[29] and brought into operation in 1981, supplying the Zavia refinery. Small-scale deposits of oil in the Hamada al-Hamrah zone in central Libya were in course of development in the late 1970s and early 1980s.

Exploration in the Libyan zones of the Mediterranean continent shelf has been pursued only tentatively so far. Sovereignty in the offshore area remained to be defined by 1981. In that year first steps had been taken to bring disputed oil-bearing offshore areas for ajudication before the International Court of Justice.[30] Potential disputes with Malta, Italy and other countries affecting the offshore zone served to constrain Libyan exploration of the offshore shelf.

The position of Libya in respect of published proved reserves of crude oil as estimated by Opec is shown in Table 1. At 23,000 million barrels, Libyan reserves would last for 36 years at present rates of output.

Development of the Libyan Oil Industry

Table 1: Proven oil reserves in Libya 1961-80 (million barrels)

1961	3,000	1971	25,000
1962	4,500	1972	30,400
1963	7,000	1973	25,500
1964	9,000	1974	26,600
1965	10,000	1975	26,700
1966	20,000	1976	25,500
1967	29,200	1977	25,000
1968	30,000	1978	24,300
1969	35,000	1979	23,500
1970	29,200	1980	23,000

Source: Opec:1981[31]

Gas reserves in Libya are poorly defined, as might be expected in a country that has concentrated on oil production. Gas fields in western areas, offshore in the Gulf of Surt, and in the south east have all been discovered but not yet developed. Esso exploited gas fields in Concessions 6 and 20 in the Surt Basin. Reserves of natural gas were estimated at $674,000$ million cubic metres on January 1, 1981.[32]

EXPLOITATION OF HYDROCARBONS

Within the Surt Basin there are eight major petroleum operations as defined by company interests. The following break-down of these operations provides details of the way nationalisation affected the various oil companies and describes the extensive pipeline network.[33]

    1. Oil was found in commercial quantities in the Zelten field by Esso Libya in 1959 at depths of between 5,465 and 5,665 feet five years after the company had begun exploration activities in the country. Marsa el Breqa was developed as an oil terminal from 1960 linked by a 175 kilometre 30-inch crude pipeline to Zelten. Esso Libya was responsible for the first export of Libyan crude in 1961. Smaller fields, Riah and Jabel were tied into the pipeline system later. The Libyan government held a 51 per cent share in Esso Libya following the general nationalisation decree of September 1973 and Esso's acquiescence in it in April 1974. Esso

announced its withdrawal from this and its other Libyan operations in November 1981 and reached a compensation agreement with the Libyan National Oil Company (LNOC) in January 1982.
2. Esso Sirte was granted Concessions 16, 17, and 20 in December 1955 and oil was found in commercial quantities at Raguba. Oil was evacuated by means of a 90 kilometre 20-inch spur to the Esso Libya line leading to Marsa el Breqa. The company was owned 63.5 per cent by the government, 24.5 per cent by Exxon (prior to November 1982 when its share was purchased by the national oil company) and 12 per cent by Grace. An original holding of 25.5 per cent by Atlantic Richfield was taken over by the Libyan government in February 1974, when all Esso Sirte companies relinquished 51 per cent of their shares to LNOC
3. For long the largest oil producer in Libya, the Oasis Oil Company began production in 1962. Crude oil was drawn from the Gialo, Defa, Dahra, and Bahi oilfields via an 850 kilometre trunkline of 1 million b/d capacity to the es Sider oil terminal. Ownership of the concession was 59.2 per cent LNOC, with Marathon and Conoco holding 16.3 per cent each and Amerada Hess 8.2 per cent. Shell, an original 16.7 per cent partner in Oasis refused to accept the 1973 nationalisation and its share was seized by the government in 1974.
4. Occidental Libya was a late entrant to operations and its first commercial production did not begin until 1968, though after that date it rapidly assumed a substantial role as an exporter of crude. Production took place mainly from the Intisar and Augila fields in Concessions 102 and 103. A pipeline network of approximately 270 kilometres joined the fields and evacuated crude oil to a terminal at Zuwaytinah. Occidental's dependence on Libyan supplies for a substantial part of its crude oil supply was used as a bargaining lever by LNOC in its efforts to change all the companies' operating conditions. In 1970 Occidental was the first to accept higher posted prices and on August 11, 1973 it acquiesced in a 51 per cent nationalisation.

Development of the Libyan Oil Industry

       Within six months of its nationalisation, Occidental signed a production-sharing agreement with LNOC covering 21 widely dispersed exploration areas. Occidental discovered two oilfields close to existing pipelines in 1976 and became entitled to 19 per cent of production from these Exploration and Production Sharing Agreement fields free of Libyan taxes and royalties.

5. Agip Libya began work in Libya under joint-venture terms with the Libyan General Petroleum Corporation (Lipetco) in the late 1960s and in 1969 announced an important find at the Abu Ateiffel field in Concession 100. Production was delayed until 1972 while Agip built both gas and oil pipelines to link up with Occidental's oilfields. In 1972 the terms of the partnership with the government were changed though Agip retained a 50, rather than the more normal 49 per cent, share in Agip Libya.

6. Mobil-Gelsenberg was owned 51 per cent by the Libyan government at the beginning of 1982 with 31.85 per cent held by Mobil and 17.15 per cent by Gelsenberg. At that time discussions were in hand for a relinquishment of ownership by Mobil. Production was concentrated in the Amal field in Concession 12 and linked via a 282 kilometre pipeline to Ras Lanuf terminal, while the Hofra and Ora fields led to the same export point through a 160 kilometre line.

7. Amoseas was a joint Texaco and Socal development in the first place but their assets were seized and later formally nationalised in February 1974. Their Nafoora oilfield was subsequently operated by the state Umm al Gawabi Company. Oil from Nafoora was conveyed by parallel 52 kilometre line to join Mobil's Amal-Ras Lanuf pipeline.

8. The Arabian Gulf Exploration Company represented a fruther part of the state machinery for production operations. The company was set up to take over the former BP-Bunker Hunt Concession 65. BP was nationalised in 1971 in apparent relatiation for the alleged failure by the United Kingdom to prevent the Iranian seizure of the islands of Abu Moosa and the Tunbs off the Arabian Peninsula. Hunt's interest was taken over in June 1973. Crude was led from the Sarir

Development of the Libyan Oil Industry

oilfield and transported via a 512 kilometre 34-inch pipeline to Marsa Hariga in Eastern Libya. A second field, Mussalla, was brought into production and a 384 kilometre 42-inch trunkline to Ras Lanuf was planned.

In addition to these large-scale operations, there were exports from Concessions 92 and 93, returned to the state, respectively, by Phillips in 1971 and Amoco in 1976. There was small production by Wintershall in Concession 96 and an Elf-Aquitaine consortium, in which Elf held 42 per cent, Hispanoil 42 per cent and Murphy 16 per cent, lifted oil from the Majid oilfield. These fields were linked into the Amal-Ras Lanuf system. The Elf consortium was untouched by nationalisation, although a joint venture between the French company and Lipetco, set up in 1968, was turned into a 15:58 ratio production-sharing agreement in 1974. This arrangement covered the Meheiririga field. Elf was among the most active of companies in forming production-sharing agreements. In 1976 it took in OMV of Austria and Wintershall within a four-year $45 million exploration commitment and in 1980 acquired five more blocks for exploration, of which one was onshore and the others offshore. A French government embargo on all oil contracts with Libya in the first months of 1981 prevented immediate implementation of operations in these new blocks.[34]

In July 1970 the local distributors, Esso, Shell and ENI, were nationalised, conferring a local marketing monopoly on the state company. The main oil refinery for domestic requirements was located at Zawiyah where capacity was 120,000 b/d. A 10,500 b/d refinery at Marsa el Breqa was operated by Esso Sirte until January 1982. The national oil company planned to set up 10,000 topping plants at Murzuq and Sarir under the 1981-85 economic plan. Export refineries were under construction in 1982 at both Ras Lanuf and Misuratah, each with a rated capacity of 220,000 b/d (See Chapter 5 Industry).[35]

Esso Sirte constructed an Liquified National Gas (LNG) plant at Marsa el Breqa in 1968 with a capacity of 345 cubic feet per day.[27] Gas was to be drawn principally from two gas fields in Concessions 6 and 20. The main pipeline was a 175 kilometre 36-inch unit from the Zelten (now Nasser) field, which was originally planned to carry seawater to the fields as part of a subsequently abandoned oilfield reinjection programme. A second supply was taken from the Raguba field via a 98 kilometre 20/22-inch spur and further sources of natural gas were

Development of the Libyan Oil Industry

available from fields owned by Oasis and Amoseas through a pipeline feeding into the Zelten system.[27] The Libyan government refused to include the LNG plant in Esso's nationalisation settlement, which left the future of natural gas exports very much in the balance.

Natural gas from the Zelten network was to be piped along the coast of the Gulf of Surt to Misuratah for use as industrial feedstock and fuel on completion of the Russian-built gasline. Consumption of large volumes of natural gas in Misuratah as well as increased use of it for reinjection programmes appeared to offer few prospects for volume exports (8 Days:1981). Gas reinjection facilities were set up early by most companies. BP and Occidental, for example, both installed field site plants in 1970 to separate Natural Gas Liquids (NGL) from natural gas, the gas later reinjected and the NGL used either to augment the stream of crude oil or, in the case of Occidental, piped separately to Zuetina for export. Oasis and Mobil installed gas reinjection wells in their oilfield area, though not all were utilized.

PRODUCTION AND CONSUMPTION

During the decade to 1980 Libyan production of crude oil dropped from 3,320,000 b/d to 1,790,000 b/d, declining at an annual average rate of 6 per cent. In the same period Libya fell from fourth largest producer in Opec to fifth and its share of world output declined from 6.9 per cent in 1970 to 2.8 per cent in 1980. Details of annual production from the start of commercial output are shown in Table 2.

The distribution of production between operating companies indicates that Oasis/LNOC consistently outproduced all others in the second half of the 1980s, only Arabian Gulf approaching Oasis in significance. For the most part, operations outside Oasis/LNOC and Arabian Gulf were very small-scale and in many cases, notably that of Esso Sirte and Esso Standard/NOC, declining (Table 3).

North America and Western Europe were the main purchasers of Libyan Crude oil throughout the 1970s. In 1979 exports of oil from Libya were directed according to Opec in the following proportions: North America 36.7 per cent, Latin America 6.8 per cent, Western Europe 50.6 per cent, Japan 0.3 per cent, the Middle East 2.2 per cent, Eastern Europe 3.3 per cent and all other 0.1 per cent. In 1981 the situation of production and exports became confused as contract customers and equity holders exercised rights to suspend liftings in protest against what were claimed to be high prices charged for Libyan crude. In these circumstances, output in October 1981 fell as low as 600,000 b/d (Financial Times:1981).[36] Table 4 shows estimates of Libyan crude oil and products export in the period 1961-1980.

Table 2: Oil production in Libya 1961-80

('000 b/d)

1961	20	1971	2,765
1962	185	1972	2,240
1963	465	1973	2,180
1964	860	1974	1,520
1965	1,225	1975	1,480
1966	1,505	1976	1,930
1967	1,745	1977	2,065
1968	2,600	1978	1,985
1969	3,110	1979	2,090
1970	3,320	1980	1,790

Source: BP Statistical Review of the World Oil Industry, various years.

Table 3: Crude oil production in Libya - by company

('000 b/d)

Company	1976	1977	1978	1979	1980	Production ceiling imposed April 1,1980
Oasis/LNOC	681.7	689.3	694.9	724.7	656.8	630.0
Arabian Gulf	303.2[c]	368.8	318.7	422.2	391.8	540.0[a]
Occidental/LNOC	321.5	345.6	340.8	329.3	240.5	190.0
Esso Standard/ LNOC	180.9	177.4	152.2	138.7	100.8	160.0[b]
AGIP/LNOC	155.5	163.2	159.6	166.1	162.5	160.0[a]
Umm al Gawabi	113.6	139.8	127.5	141.4	125.7	.....
Esso Sirte/LNOC	67.4	68.1	65.0	60.5	44.6	.....[b]
Mobil/LNOC	89.6	95.3	94.8	87.8	86.0	81.0
Aquitaine Group/ LNOC	17.5	13.6	15.9	17.0	14.3	10.0
Wintershall	1.8	2.4	3.2	4.2	3.6	4.0
	1932.7	2063.5	1982.6	2091.9	1826.6	1750.0

Source: Opec
Notes: a. Including Umm al Gawabi allowance
b. All Esso
c. Including Amoco's share of 1,400 b/d

Development of the Libyan Oil Industry

Table 4: Exports of crude oil and refined products from Libya - 1961-80

('000 b/d)

Year	Exports	Year	Exports
1961	14.4	1971	2747.4
1962	179.5	1972	2214.6
1963	459.5	1973	2209.5
1964	856.4	1974	1518.1
1965	1212.7	1975	1478.3
1966	1499.6	1976	1899.6
1967	1717.3	1977	2034.2
1968	2582.4	1978	1954.0
1969	3070.9	1979	2050.6
1970	3312.9	1980	1776.4[a]

Source: Oapec
Note: a. Estimate

Statistics concerning production of natural gas are not readily available. Production figures for 1979 and 1980 were estimated at 4,600 and 3,300 million cubic metres, respectively.[32] These figures concern commercial production and exclude gas flared or reinjected into oilfields. Export figures for the same years were 3,600 and 2,300 million cubic metres. Most exports of natural gas were conducted through long-term contracts with ENI of Italy and Catalana de Gas of Spain.

FORECASTS OF FUTURE CHANGES IN HYDROCARBON RESERVES, PRODUCTION AND EXPORTS 1981-2000

Projections of future production and export trends must be regarded with the greatest of caution. Forecasts for the oil industry made for the 1970s and early 1980s have proved to be highly erroneous. The following Table 5 presents three forecasts for Libyan production, consumption and export of crude oil during the decade 1980-1990.

Discrepancies between the forecasts for exports can be explained by the exclusion from the Speerplan/Finnmap projections of all product exports, while projections I and II in Table 5 are inclusive of exports of products. NLOC assumed steady levels of output of crude oil through to the year 2000 on the basis of indicated or desired production ceilings. Their figures for domestic consumption were consistently below those proposed even by the Opec Secretariat, shown in Table 5 incorporated in the

Development of the Libyan Oil Industry

Fesharaki forecasts. All three sources suggest production and export levels below those used in preparation of the Perspective Plan.

Table 5: Forecasts of crude oil production in Libya
('000 b/d)

		1985	1990
Production	I	1,500	1,500
	II	1,600	1,200
	III	1,000	1,000 - 750
Consumption	I	125	160
	II	170	310
	III	480	500 - 650
Exports	I	1,380	1,340
	II	1,430	890
	III	520	250 - 350

Sources: I. LNOC[37]
II. Fesharaki:1981 [38]
III. Speerplan-Finnmap: 1980 [39]

In fact, production ceilings imposed by the Libyan government became less relevant from 1980 as the balance between oil demand and supply in the international market increasingly favoured the consumers. LNOC had difficulties disposing of its crude oil during 1981 and output fell below one million b/d by the middle of the year to levels not experienced on a consistent basis since 1963/64 (Table 2).

Policy towards production levels emphasised the need to reduce output from 1980.[24] The experiences of 1981 were caused, however, by outside pressures and reduced exports of crude oil together with deteriorating unit prices for oil on the international market led to a fall in Libyan holdings of foreign exchange and a call for greater financial stringency on the budgets of government departments.[40] Initiatives on oil prices taken elsewhere in Opec became more important influences on Libyan ability to dispose of given levels of crude oil than decisions on the matter taken within the country.

Difficulties in selling Libyan crudes at prices acceptable to the national oil company and the government during 1980 and 1981 served to undermine previous and possibly over-ambitious plans for Libyan crude oil output rising to 2.5 million b/d in the period 1980-1990. Constraints on oil exports, while creating the need for some financial

Development of the Libyan Oil Industry

adjustments in October 1981, when Libyan agencies first looked for external sources of funding, did have the virtue of enforcing conservation of Libyan oil reserves. The state was forced to practice its publicly proclaimed policies of protecting the country's position on oil reserves, a concordance not generally to be observed in earlier years.

There has been much debate in recent years concerning published proved reserves. Opec's figures for proven crude oil reserves in 1980 was 23,000 million barrels, representing some 5.3 per cent of total reserves held by Opec members. (This compared with a 1969 figure of 35,000 million barrels or 8.8 per cent of the Opec total). In 1980 the production-to-reserves ratio was 1:36. Recovery factors from fields in Libya differed radically, with Occidental's Intisar field revealing an 85 per cent recovery factor against a number of fields which had been assigned recovery factors as low as 20 per cent of oil in place (MEES, 1979). In 1981 Libya announced a three year pilot programme, to begin in 1982, to determine the most efficient enhanced recovery methods for the country's oil fields. Officially the plan is to spend £1 billion in the period 1985-2000 on increasing recoverable oil reserves from their present level to 32,000 million barrels. Authorities in Tripoli have placed their hopes in improving recovery factors on existing fields which are estimated to have total reserves of 75,000 million barrels of oil in place (MEED, 1981). Clearly the discovery of new oil fields once the offshore zone is fully opened to exploration would also be essential for Libya to maintain a high reserves position into the next century.

The apparently strong reserves position of Libya can be misleading. Technical constraints on output from oilfields were becoming more severe in the early 1980s. Problems of reservoir management were acknowledged by the Secretary for Oil Affairs in 1979 to have forced a reduced target for production in that year from 2.4 million b/d to 2.18 million b/d. It was later confirmed that output from existing oilfields would fall gradually to 1.3 to 1.4 million b/d by 1985.[25] While the demands of conservation were important in reducing forecasts for oil production during the early 1980s, it was increasingly apparent that management of oilfields was proving difficult and that recovery techniques were not stimulating so marked an improvement in output as had been expected. Particular emphasis was placed on encouraging new exploration after 1980.

Development of the Libyan Oil Industry

In 1981 fifteen agreements were negotiated with overseas companies for production-sharing operations. The Secretariat of Oil announced at that time that its objective had become to locate as much crude as was to be produced over the decade to 1990.

Urgent requirement for discovery of new oil bearing areas was enhanced by fears that existing reserves would increasingly be taken up to cater for domestic demand for oil and products. Domestic consumption of crude stood at 130,000 b/d in 1979 and rose to 140,000 b/d in 1980. A combination of rising living standards, increasing industrialisation, greater use of energy-intensive processes in agriculture and high energy costs of water provision, suggested that domestic use of oil would rise steeply to reach 480,000 b/d by 1985 and 650,00 b/d by 1990.[28] LNOC estimates indicated that domestic consumption of crude as feedstock for domestic refineries would rise to 600,000 b/d, to give a total consumption figure in the region of 775,000 b/d by the late 1980s. Figure 4 suggests the range of possibilities for trends in production and domestic consumption for the period 1979-1990 as proposed by available forecasts. Radical change in these projections would be needed should large discoveries by made of new reserves.

The economic implications of a much reduced potential for crude oil exports, which would be the outcome of trends sketched in Figure 4, p 36 could be serious. In 1981 effectively no more than ten per cent of Gross Domestic Product was attributed to activities based on renewable resources. The remaining proportion of economic contributions arose from government spending on wages, projects, subsidies and other items within the ordinary, development and defence budgets,[41] almost all of which were generated by the oil sector either directly or indirectly. A marked decline in the government's access to oil revenues would diminish its abilities to fund growth within the domestic economy and limit its use of foreign exchange to finance imports of goods and services. The problems would be mitigated or worsened by the degree of success or failure in commercial exports of the refineries and petrochemical plants that will in future consume so large a proportion of the country's oil output.

While it is possible to over-state the urgency of the economic situation emerging in Libya as a result of changes in the oil sector, it is none the less clear that the general trend in the future will be for declining volumes of oil exports. Essentially, the country's period as a crude oil exporting rentier

Development of the Libyan Oil Industry

state will draw to a close. New sources of state income, foreign exchange earnings and employment will be needed. Structural changes in the economy and the nature of the labour force will be required to make Libya reliant on productive sectors such as agriculture, manufacturing industry and commerce before the end of the century. Adjustment of this kind, especially if rushed, could prove a severe test for so early developing a state with such a narrow range of renewable resources.

Notes

1. Ghanem, S., 1975, *The pricing of Libyan crude oil*, Adams Publishing House, Malta
2. Waddams, F., 1980, *The Libyan oil industry*, Croom Helm, London
3. United Nations, 1979, *National physical perspective plan 1981-2000*, Tripoli
4. Sharaf, A.E.R., 1963, *The geography of the kingdom of Libya*, Elmasri Press, Alexandria, p 602 (in Arabic)
5. Petroleum Law No 25/1955, May 1955, *Official Gazette*
6. Petroleum Commission, *Petroleum Development of Libya*, 1944-1961, 1961, Government Press, p 18
7. OPEC 1973, *Annual Review and record*, Information Department, Vienna, p 14
8. Royal Decree amending *The Petroleum Law of 1955*, July 15, 1961, *Official Gazette* of the United Kingdom of Libya, Tripoli, Article 13, paragraph (1) C
9. The protest was announced by the Chairman of the Libyan Petroleum Commission on July 12, 1961 *The Economist*, October 28, 1961, London, p 369
10. The Economist wrote that it was perhaps significant that the oil company "mentions the quality and not the gravity" *The Economist*, August 12, 1961
11. OPEC, *Resolution No IV 33*, November 1964, Information Department, Vienna (The seventh OPEC Conference held in Djakarta) See also OTAIBA, M.S. Al, 1975, *OPEC and the petroleum industry*, Croom Helm, p 141
12. *Royal Decree amending the Petroleum Law of 1955*, issued November 9, 1961, December 6 1961, *Official Gazette* of the United Kingdom of Libya, No 17
13. Hangari, I., Under-secretary of the Libyan Ministry of Petroleum Affairs, December 8 1968, issued *Petroleum Regulation No 8* (not published in

in the official gazette)

14. *OPEC 18th Conference of OPEC*, Bagdad, November 1968, Information Department, Vienna

15. Ghanem, S., 1975, *The pricing of Libyan crude oil*, Adams Publishing House, Malta, Appendix No 7, Tripoli Agreement March 20 1971, p 326-332. See also *Middle East Economic Survey* April 2 1971 and the *Supplement* April 9 1971; *Oil Agreement*, January 1973, Arabian Gulf Exploration Company, Benghazi, p 3-13; *Petroleum Intelligence Weekly, Special Supplement*, April 5, 1971 and April 9 1971

16. *Ministry of Petroleum*, October 20, 1970, *Technical Department Publication*; See also Ghanem, S., 1975, *The pricing of Libyan crude oil*, see table 36, summary of cut backs of crude oil production ordered by the Ministry of Petroleum

17. Ghanem, S. 1975, *The pricing of Libyan crude oil*, Table 37, increase of the Libyan crude oil posted price (40° API) as a result of September 1 1970 Agreement, p 155

18. For a full text of the Tehran Agreement see Ghanem, S., 1975, *The pricing of Libyan crude oil*, Appendix No 6, Teheran Price Agreement, February 14 1971, p 326-332. See also *Middle East Economic Survey*, February 19 1971; *Petroleum Intelligence Weekly*, February 22, 1971

19. Ministry of Petrolum, Libyan Arab Republic 1973, *Libyan Oil*, 1954-1971, Tripoli

20. Ghanem, S.,1975, *The pricing of Libyan crude oil*, p 214, Table 56, posted price increases after 1973 October war in the Middle East, p 216;217, and p 223. See also *Petroleum Intelligence Weekly*, October 7 1973, January 7; 21, and 28, 1974, Beirut, pp 1, 9, 9 and 11

21. Ghanem, S., 1975, *The pricing of Libyan crude oil*, Appendix No 12, Text of Law Nationalising 51 per cent of the oil companies' assets in Libya, September 1973, p 359-366. See also *Supplement to the Middle East Economic Survey*, September 14 1973, Beirut, p 2-7

22. Waddams,F., 1980, *The Libyan oil industry*, 13.3 Exploration, drilling and production, p 284-288 and Table 13.4 drilling activities in Libya, 1969-1976, p 284. See also 1969-71 *Ministry of Petroluem*; 1972-1976 *Central Bank of Libya*, March/April 1977, Economic Bulleten

23. Waddams, F., 1980, *The Libyan oil industry*, 12.9 production-sharing joint ventures, p 260-263

24. *Middle East Economic Survey*, March 24 1980, 23/22 Libya cuts production ceiling by 350,000 b/d See also *Middle East Economic Survey*, April 20 1981,

Development of the Libyan Oil Industry

24/36 Libyan Oil Minister calls for radical revision of OPEC's long-term strategy price-plan
26. United Nations, 1979, *National physical perspective plan 1981-2000*, Tripoli p 25
27. Waddams, F., 1980, *The Libyan oil industry*, 9.3 utilisation of gas, p 199-200
28. Speerplan, 1980, *El Khalij Region; existing conditions 1979 and regional potential*, Frankfurt, AM
29. Waddams, F., 1980, *The Libyan oil industry*, 9.2 pipelines and terminals, p 198-9
30. Government of Libya, May 30 1981, *Memorials*, submitted to the International Court of Justice by the Socialist People's Arab Jamahiriya
31. OPEC, 1981, *OPEC Annual Statistical Bulletin*, Information Department, Vienna
32. *Petroleum Economist*, August 1981, XLVII/7 *Natural Gas - World Survey*, p 335-339
33. General references for section entitled Exploitation of Hydrocarbons:- Kubbah, A.A.Q., 1964, *Libya - its oil industry and economic system*, Rihani Press, Beirut; Waddams, F., 1980, *The Libyan oil industry*, 4.2 exploration activities p 73-79 and Table 4.2 undertakings of conditions outside the terms of the law by oil companies obtaining new concessions and assignments, Appendix 4.1 chronological list of concessions award from November 1955-April 1961, and reference 20
34. *Middle East Economic Survey*, July 20 1981, 24/39, France lifts embargo on dealings with Libya
35. Waddams, F., 1980, *The Libyan oil industry*, 9.4 refining and marketing of oil production in Libya, p 200-204
36. Financial Times, *Mid-East Markets*, November 2 1981, 8/22, p11
37. *Middle East Economic Survey*, September 28 1981, LNOC forecasts
38. Fesharaki, F., 1981 World oil available: the role of OPEC policies, *Annual Review of Energy*, Vol 6
39. Speerplan/Finnmap 1981, Draft regional plan 1980-2000, Frankfurt AM
40. *Middle East Economic Digest*, September 18-24 1981, 25/38, Congress urges economies to beat world oil glut, *Jamahiriyah Review*, February 1982, p 28
41. Stauffer, T.R. September 7 1981, Measuring oil addiction, a paper based on a lecture given to the Arab Planning Unit in Kuwait and published in *Middle East Economic Survey*

Chapter 5
THE DEVELOPMENT OF LIBYAN INDUSTRY

P.Barker

INTRODUCTION

Following the failure of Libyan agriculture during the 1970s to respond to many of the impossible demands made of it, pole position in the country's drive for economic diversification is now unequivocally occupied by the industrial sector, both for light and heavy industry. Projected expenditure figures for the second Transformation Plan (1981-85) reveal industry's allocation at LD4 bn compared with agriculture's LD3 bn. And while Libya's poor implementation record during previous plans suggests that these sums may have little final relationship to reality, there is no doubting the decision and determination of the country's leadership to shift the emphasis of economic development. Industrialisation, especially with a bias towards heavy industry, has a natural appeal for a country undergoing its own version of socialist transformation, but rhetoric and broad policy statements can be no substitute for a coherent strategy aimed at maximising the advantages of Libya's current capital surplus to create a sector that will provide employment opportunities, treasury revenues and foreign exchange earnings after oil exports have diminished drastically or ceased altogether.
    After a brief historical description of Libya's meagre industrial experience to date, this chapter will examine the country's planned industrial projects to see whether there is evidence of an industrial strategy or whether, as in the case of agriculture, the government might be accused of having deceived itself into thinking that high spending on isolated projects constitutes a strategy.[1] Particular attention will be paid to Libya's petrochemical and processed metal products' future inter-

national competitiveness and marketability, and also to the social and infrastructural demands of the new industrial projects.

HISTORICAL BACKGROUND

The Italians were the first to introduce modern industry into Libya during their period of control (1911-43). Statistics show that by 1938, 789 establishments were in existence, making basic goods for consumption in the country. These factories were almost all small in size and were situated in Tripoli, Benghazi, Darnah or Misuratah. Four out of five were owned by Italians. According to El Mehdawi, the more important establishments were those which produced building materials, metal products, agricultural foodstuffs and tobacco. Although many of the original factories were destroyed, during the war, much the same light industrial structure emerged during the 1950s but with more local ownership. During the 1950s two industrial training centres were established in Tripoli and Benghazi and, according to a 1956 census, there were then 3121 industrial establishments in Libya, 87 per cent of which employed fewer than 10 people.[2]

In 1961 Libya's first Ministry of Industry was created and manufacturing was also accorded official recognition in the first five-year development plan (1963-68) with a 3 per cent share of the total planned development expenditure of LD169 mn. Industry's share was to have risen to 7.9 per cent of the LD980 mn planned expenditure in the 1969-74 plan, which was only operational for five months. Actual disbursement of government funds to industry was very low in the 1960s in value terms and in relation to other sectors. Sayigh estimates the percentage of actual to planned investment in industry in 1968 and 1969 at 15.6 per cent and 8.9 per cent respectively. He notes that actual investment in industry reached a reasonably high level only in 1971, with a 62.8 per cent disbursement of a planned total of LD32 mn, and calculates that in what might be called Libya's first industrial decade (1962-71) the rise in industrial value added was 142.7 per cent at current prices but only 21.0 per cent at constant 1964 prices.[3] The pre-revolutionary government restricted its direct investment in the industrial sector to less than 10 establishments, although it did create the Real Estate and Industrial Bank in 1965, which in the period up to September

1970 lent LD11.7 mn.[4]

After the 1969 revolution the attitude in government to industry changed dramatically as more attention was paid to the development of public sector projects. In 1970 the National Public Organisation for Industrialisation (NPOI) was established as the major organ for implementing the public sector's industrial development plan. Initial capital of NPOI was put at LD6 mn but this has been increased many-fold in succeeding years. It its first year of operation NPOI was involved in five projects, by 1977 the number had risen to 43, and by 1980 NPOI was to have funded 91 projects with a total capital investment of LD500 mn.[5] The rising value of planned and actual government investment in Libya's industrial sector that occurred after the Revolution is shown clearly in table 1

Table 1: Government investment in the development of the Libyan industrial sector, 1965-76 (LD mn)

	Planned	Actual
1965-66	4.3	2.0
1966-67	5.8	4.7
1967-68	5.3	7.4
1968-69	7.7	5.0
1969-70	7.9	5.4
1970-71	20.9	15.0
1971-72	37.0	29.0
1972-73	68.1	65.1
1973	79.7	67.5
1974	133.7	135.4
1975	129.7	117.6
1976	199.4	152.1

Source: Secretary of Industry, *The Achievements of the Revolution in the Industrial Sector* 1977

Increased government expenditure on industry until 1976 was accompanied by a corresponding decline in private sector investment; local entrepreneurs were "scared off by the RCC's (Revolutionary Command Council) ill-defined attitude towards the private sector".[6] In 1968 private sector investment in manufacturing was valued at LD4.2 mn compared to public capital funding of LD0.9 mn. Although by 1972 private sector investment had risen to LD7.8 mn, the government in this year pumped LD11.7 mn into industry. In subsequent years direct private sector investment has fallen away completely.⁷ The role of the industrial bank, which had previously been a major lender to the private ccnstruction industry and food processing sector, has also declined in recent years, and in 1981 its real estate operations were taken up by a new Real Estate Investment and Savings Bank established to encourage "construction and personal savings linked to property".⁸ Private construction has undoubtedly remained more buoyant than activity in any other industrial subsector, but even here the effects of Resolution Four of May (Resolution Four: the resolution of the General People's Congress announcing the beginning of socialist control of the country) and subsequent rulings on property and houses have proved enervating. The introduction of government investment in industry on a large scale has also had the quite deliberate result of redressing the previous heavy bias in favour of small scale industrial establishments.

The promulgation of the first Plan of Economic and Social Transformation (1976-80) represents a watershed in the development of Libyan industry. 19 per cent of planned investment was allocated to the industrial sector, with this leap being made possible by the important change in investment priorities towards major capital intensive heavy industry projects.⁹ Libya's commitment to heavy industry was announced to the world at large, slightly prematurely perpaps in view of the fact that many of the proposed projects have had to be rolled over to the 1981-85 plan for completion or, worse still, for commencement. Libya's determination to industrialise is even more firmly stamped on the 1981-85 plan, the second Plan of Economic and Social Transformation, in the form of a 21.5 per cent leading investment allocation.¹⁰ The subsectoral breakdown in table 2 shows that the industrial groups (metallurgy and petrochemicals, in particular) are to be the main recipients of this huge capital expenditure.

Despite the huge investments that are being poured into industry by the Libyan government, tables 3 and 4 show that manufacturing has yet to register a significant return on this capital in terms either of value added or job creation. The situation is supposed to change by 1985 when it is planned that the oil sector's contribution to GDP will have fallen to 47 per cent. It is therefore during the present decade that Libya's industrial programme will come under the closest scrutiny.¹¹

The Development of Libyan Industry

Table 2: Investment by industry groups during 1981-1985

Industry group	Total 1981-1985 (in $m)	Structure (per cent)	Growth rate 1981-1985 (per cent)
Food industries	536.4	6.2	16.4
Textiles and leather	223.6	2.6	16.3
Wood and furniture	6.8	-	7.6
Paper and printing	25.3	-	9.7
Chemicals	657.7	7.6	35.2
Petroleum products	837.7	9.6	21.1
Petrochemicals	2,195.4	25.3	38.9
Building materials	702.3	8.1	13.9
Metallurgy	2,742.9	31.7	60.0
Metalworking, engineering and electrical equipment	609.7	7.0	28.9
Other manufacturing industries	168.9	1.9	3.4
Total	8,706.7	100.0	21.6

Source: Draft Plan, Secretariat of Planning, Tripoli

Table 3: Employment in Libya by economic sector (per cent)

Sector	1964	1968	1973	1976	1978
Agriculture, forestry and fishing	37.0	32.5	24.1	19.3	19.1
Mining and quarrying	3.0	4.3	2.8	2.5	2.6
Manufacturing	6.8	8.4	4.8	5.1	6.1
Electricity, gas and water	1.5	1.8	1.9	1.9	2.0
Construction	7.7	11.7	16.2	22.9	21.2
Trade, restaurants and hotels	6.4	7.4	7.3	7.1	6.1
Transport, storage and communications	5.6	8.3	8.4	7.9	8.7
Finance, insurance, real estate and business	-	-	1.2	1.1	1.2
Community, social and personal services	-	-	25.3	24.0	24.7
Other services and activities not adequately defined	31.9	25.6	8.0	8.2	8.0
Total (rounded)	100.0	100.0	100.0	100.0	100.0

Source: For 1964 and 1968, Y Sayigh, *Economics of the Arab World*, Croom Helm, 1978, p464: For 1973, 1976 1978, *United Nations Industrial Handbook* (figures include Libyan and non-Libyan workers)

Table 4: Distribution of GDP at current prices by sector

	1958 LD mn	%	1962 LD mn	%	1971 LD mn	%	1975 LD mn	%	1978 LD mn	%
Agriculture, forestry and fishing	13.6	26.1	14.9	9.6	32.9	2.2	84.5	2.3	95.5	1.7
Mining and quarrying	7.2	13.8	38.6	24.8	922.7	62.8	1,980.4	53.9	3,302.4	58.8
Manufacturing	6.0	11.5	9.0	5.8	25.0	1.7	66.1	1.8	123.6	2.2
Construction	1.8	3.4	10.3	6.6	100.1	6.8	433.6	11.8	595.3	10.6
Electricity, gas and water	0.8	1.5	0.9	0.6	7.3	0.5	18.4	0.5	23.7	0.6
Transport and communications	2.9	5.6	8.6	5.5	63.7	4.3	176.4	4.8	219.0	3.9
Wholesale and retail trade	7.3	14.0	14.2	9.1	60.8	4.1	224.1	6.1	292.0	5.2
Banking and insurance	–		1.7	1.1	11.6	0.8	99.2	2.7	146.0	2.6
Public administration	6.7	12.8	15.5	10.0	100.8	6.9	257.2	7.0	359.5	6.4
Education	(a)		5.0	3.2	43.4	3.0	121.3	3.3	174.1	3.1
Health	(a)		2.1	1.4	19.1	1.3	51.4	1.4	78.6	1.4
Ownership of dwellings	5.9	11.3	29.4	18.9	66.9	4.6	132.2	3.6	157.3	2.8
Other services	(a)		5.3	3.4	14.3	1.0	29.4	0.8	39.3	0.7
GDP at factor cost	52.0	100.0	155.5	100.0	1,468.6	100.0	3,674.2	100.0	5,616.3	100.0

(a) included under 'Ownership of dwellings'

Source: For 1958, *Statistical Abstract of Libya 1958-62*; for other years, *National Accounts 1962-71 and 1971-77*

The Development of Libyan Industry

HEAVY INDUSTRY

Despite Libya's plans for heavy industry the actual heavy industrial stock in the country at the time of writing - the beginning of the 1981-85 plan - was minimal. The only major oil refinery was at Zawiyah west of Tripoli, with a capacity of 120,000 b/d. LPG and LNG exports were possibilities as a result of installations built by Esso and Occidental in the 1968-72 period,[12] although in the case of LNG pricing difficulties with customers had seriously reduced sales.[13] The two spearheads of the nascent petrochemical industry were to be found in Bregah - a 1,000 tons a day methanol plant commissioned in 1977 and working at full capacity in mid 1981, and a 1,000 tons a day ammonia plant which started producing for export in 1980 but which was experiencing operating and marketing problems in anticipation of a twin urea plant inaugurated by Colonel Qadhaffi in September 1981.[14] Near the Tunisian border the West German-built $500 mn Abu Kammash chemical complex should have been working to capacity, but an expatriate management team was left keeping the complex ticking over as the Libyan trainees had been drafted into military service coincidentally as the plant came onstream.[15]

Against these humble and faltering beginnings can be now ranged the full gamut of plants throughout Libya that are either close to completion, under construction, or at the advanced study stage. At Bregah another 1,000 tons a day ammonia plant is under construction for completion in 1982,[16] and contracts were signed in 1981 for a second urea plant at 1,750 tons a day and a second 1,000 tons a day methanol unit.[17] Along the coast at Ras Lanuf a 220,000 b/d refinery is nearing completion and a 330,000 tons a year ethylene steam cracker is under construction.[18] Also contracted for Ras Lanuf are a 52,800 tons a year monoethylene glycol plant, a 68,000 tons a year polypropylene plant, and a 55,000 tons a year low density polyethylene unit.[19] At Surt a huge new fertiliser complex is being designed, with ammonia capacity of 2,700 tons a day from two units and urea production capacity of 3,000 tons a day, also from two plants; additional capacity for compound fertilisers, nitric acid and ammonia nitrate is envisaged, and in the metallurgical sector a smelting plant is foreseen.[20] At Misuratah a 1.1 m tons a year iron and steel complex is under construction and another 220,000 b/d refinery is about to be ordered.[21] At Zuwarah, west of Tripoli, contracts have been let for a 120,000 tons a year aluminium smelter and a 170,000 tons a year petroleum coke plant.[22] Finally, three new 1 mn tons a year cement plants are at various stages of completion in Labdah, Zliten and Darnah, to augment present capacity of 1.5 mn tons a year.[23]

Certain of the key economic assumptions behind Libya's industrialisation programme can be stated simply enough and, as such, are consistent with those adopted by almost all oil and gas producing developing countries. A further question remains as to whether the implications of these key assumptions synchronise with particular Libyan political and strategic considerations. Evaluation of the industrial plan should also be carried to the individual plant level where vital decisions on product profile and volume capacity are made.

Refining oil locally for export is intended to increase the return to Libya per unit of hydrocarbon exported, which in turn should reduce the need for high crude exports to fund the country's budget and so extend the life of Libya's oil reservers. In the case of gas the various options are complicated by the essential difference between associated and non-associated gas, and by the fact that certain industrial processes use gas as both feedstock and fuel (petrochemicals) while there is a range of energy intensive industries that require the gas merely as fuel (aluminium, iron and steel, and cement production). As with oil, the basic aim in processing gas locally is to maximise domestic value added to that gas and to improve the return to Libya per hydrocarbon unit produced or exported. The opportunity to benefit economically from the harnessing of associated gas that would otherwise be flared is considerable, and both the petrochemical and energy intensive industries offer a viable alternative to trade in LNG which is expensive and underdeveloped worldwide. The comparative advantage of the energy intensive industries is less marked than that of the petrochemical industries, and may in certain cases like cement production argue for domestic production to save hard currency but against export.[24] It is generally advised that non-associated gas be used more sparingly as the option always remains for the producing country to keep this at present undervalued fuel source in the ground.

Another important assumption behind the industrialisation programme adopted by Libya is that it will play an important role in the area of employment, both quantitatively and qualitatively. Although

The Development of Libyan Industry

heavy industry is by nature capital intensive, there is always a high ratio of auxiliary and service workers to technicians in this sector in contast to the situation in agriculture. Qualitatively, if Libyans are trained successfully to operate the industrial plants, it will create a cadre of well educated and modern thinking nationals as well as redressing the heavy bias in favour of jobs in the services rather than productive sectors.

The major implication of Libya's industrialisation programme is its promise of continued interdependence with the industrialised world, and particularly Europe. The export orientation of its industrial plans contrasts markedly with the more isolationist, self-sufficient philosophy behind the country's agricultural projects and "Green Revolution" and will have important consequences for the spatial development of modern Libya. All the new industrial projects are being located on the Mediterranean coast to miminise the overland transport costs of plant imports and product exports, to maximise the freight advantage of Libya's proximity to the European market, and to be next to the only readily available source of cooling water, the sea. Industrialisation therefore effectively reduces Libya's chances of creating new population centres inland, and asserts the country's Mediterranean rather than African credentials. It is not clear that the Libyan authorities yet fully understand the geographic, trade and economic imperatives of their new industries. For instance the plan to provide iron for the Misuratah works from the distant and underdeveloped Fezzan mining region seems to hark back to the ideas of self-sufficiency and integration rather than acknowledge the new and harsh economic realities of the world's iron and steel industry where gas producers are advised generally to use imported scrap as feedstock.[25]

In a similar vein, if Libya wished, as has recently been mooted, to build up an economically viable atomic energy generating industry, it would clearly be best counselled to import uranium for any site planned on the coast rather than harbour ideas of developing its own uranium mine in the isolated south of the country.[26]

There are other instances where Libya's industrial plans, as currently expounded, suggest a tendency to overlook the high cost of internal travel and transport in the interests of greater integration of the country's regions and towards the aim of breaking the duopoly of Tripoli and Benghazi as population centres.²⁷ Unfortunately Libya's economic advantage over its competitors, especially in the energy intensive industries, is not so great as to allow heavy industry to take the strain of radical population dispersal. The industrial plans for Misuratah and Surt are both, for instance, contingent on the building of the so-called "Russian gas pipeline" along the coast westwards from Bregah. Apart from the initial capital costs of the pipeline which might be expected to be recovered via end-user charges, there will also be relatively heavy operation and maintenance charges which could erode much of the fuel advantage enjoyed by the Misuratah iron and steel works. A similar argument could be induced to question the advisability of extending the proposed Sarir water pipeline along the coast from Bregah-Ras Lanuf to Surt. On the other hand it is clear that it would be impossible to build all the planned industries at Bregah-Ras Lanuf at the end of the pipelines up from the south. Already it is feared that the manpower explosion required to implement planned projects - and to give an estimated end-century population for the two towns of 130,000 - may be unrealisable and lead to an enforced slow down in project implementation.²⁸ This will certainly be the case if Libya abandons its present lenient attitude to the presence of expatriate workers.

Building up an adequate human and physical infrastructure for the industrialisation programme presents Libya with an unenviable dilemma. It is clear that, if industry is to be self-sustaining and competitive, overhead costs of utilities such as electricity and water must be kept to a minimum. Present indications are that the lack of a fixed hierarchy for economic decision making in Libya will lead to a duplication of effort in these areas between higher committees, secretariats, and even foreign contractors and consultants, and that satisfactory economies of scale will not be realised.

If Libyan industry is unable to run without subsidies from the general budget, it will clearly not have satisfied its major objective of providing an alternative source of income to crude oil exports. It is therefore encouraging to note a new realism in government attitudes towards capital investments. In an interview in September 1981 the Secretary for Heavy Industry Omar Muntassa revealed that new monitoring units were to be established within both the Heavy and Light Industry Secretariats to ensure maximum benefit from invested capital, maximum

The Development of Libyan Industry

operational capacity, and to avoid the construction of new factories with built-in technological and/or economic deficiencies.[29] Not all the problems, however, can be simply wished away. It is almost inevitable, for instance, that the heavy industrial plants will be asked to bear more of the burden of job creation than a capital-intensive industry should do; and staff will be on the payroll who never turn up for work or who are away on military service.[30]

A multitude of unknowns makes it impossible to construct an accurate balance sheet for any of the future heavy industrial plants. Feedstock costs, utility costs, the size of the labour force, and the proposed rate of capital recovery are all either carefully kept secrets or have yet to be decided. Some broad range of profitability criteria can be devised, however, bearing in mind the basic economic assumptions and taking into account both local and international market factors. In general the oil and gas producing countries are considered capable of maximising their cheap feedstock gains in the production of simple petrochemicals; the further downstream the production process goes, the less relative weighting is given to feedstock costs. On the other hand because it is in the field of simple "building block" petrochemicals that the world market is most competitive, it is essential for new export plants to be as large as the latest technology allows in order to effect essential economies of scale.

A comparision of Libyan industrial plans with those of Saudi Arabia, which is embarked on a similar and competitive programme, should help to identify some of the potential problems and advantages of individual Libyan projects. In the first place it should be made clear that, whereas Saudi Arabia intends to use the various fractions of its associated gas (methane, ethane, LPG and NGLs) separately, Libya has so far indicated no intention of separating out its fractions in a similar fashion. Libya is therefore restricted to using its gas as feedstock and fuel for the production of ammonia and methanol and as fuel alone in energy intensive projects; its ethylene is to be produced from naptha. Methanol is produced under less severe conditions than ammonia, and Libya has had considerable success with its first methanol plant. A capacity of 365,000 tons a year is small, however, compared to Saudi Arabia's two planned plants at 650,000 tons a year and 600,000 tons a year respectively, and the new methanol unit for Bregah, with the same capacity as the first, it clearly necessary to maintain Libya's competitiveness.[31] Demand for methanol is growing faster than that for other petrochemicals, and market entry is facilitated for the new producer by virtue of the fact that 40 per cent of total sales take place on the merchant market.

Libya's investment in ammonia and urea production is considerable. The size of of plant, first at Bregah and then as planned for Surt, is keeping pace with new technology, and as urea is much easier to transport than ammonia, the twinning of production units is good policy. There could be some difficulty in individual marketing of 1.5 mn tons of urea a year, especially if there is a preference shift among farmers away from urea to other fertilisers. The main doubts about the Surt fertiliser plants as well as about the Misuratah iron and steel works are those mentioned above and relate to their location away from the feedstock and fuel source. Similarly it seems strange to locate an export refinery at Misuratah which is not connected to any oil field by pipeline.

The Libyan decision to produce ethylene from the naptha cut of its Ras Lanuf refinery is decidedly more controversial and contrary to modern trends, which have shown a marked preference for ethylene production from ethane rather than naptha cracking. In Saudi Arabia three ethane crackers are planned with annual production capacities of 656,000 tons a year, 450,000 tons a year, and 500,000 tons a year compared with the 330,000 tons a year envisaged from the Ras Lanuf plant. The real difference in the two processes, however, concerns the production of other less marketable olefins. Ethylene yield from naptha reaches a maximum 30 per cent at a temperature of 650° C, with significant quantities of propylene, butene, and butadiene also being produced. If ethane is the feedstock, the ethylene yield is likely to reach 75-80 per cent.[32] The Ras Lanuf complex will therefore have to handle a larger number of chemicals in smaller quantities, especially as the refinery is also to be equipped with a catalytic reformer producing volumes of aromatics.[33] The Libyans have almost forced themselves at Ras Lanuf into creating a fully articulated chemical complex, which contradicts the apparent strategy of simple production units found in Bregah, Surt and even Abu Kammash where the four production units are all mutually independent. Moreover several of the likely products (carbon black, polybutadiene) have strictly limited export potential. The Ras Lanuf operating costs are certain to escalate with the complexities and number of plant, and the net gain in the case of ethylene and other by-products has to be gauged against the export price not of crude or gas, but of naptha.

Comparision of Libya's heavy industrial plans with those of Saudi Arabia pinpoints a vital difference in management and marketing strategies. Simply, Saudi Arabia has formed joint venture partnerships for all its refinery, petrochemical and metallurgy projects which place the onus for maketing on the foreign partner and also ensure the latter's interest in the profitability of the project.[34] Director of the Saudi Basic Industries Corporation (Sabic) Abdulaziz al-Zamil is in no doubt that "the ability of partners to commit themselves to the marketing of the products of the joint venture is the most essential factor in ensuring the viability of the project".[35] The Libyans have on the other hand adopted with minor adjustments the turnkey approach despite warnings that marketing may constitute Libya's major problem. The Libyans are, however, now asking contractors to provide operational and technical assistance in running plants after completion. This kind of assistance is not popular with contractors as it is difficult to cost within an overall bid, nor does it touch on the marketing aspects.[36]

LIGHT INDUSTRY

The development of light industry during the 1980s should present less of a challenge to Libyan officials. Although it is the intention to export some of the produce from the new range of larger factories currently coming onstream, the main thrust of local industry will be either import substitution, or, as traditionally, the processing of local raw materials for consumption or for building. It is definitely the intention of government to try and sponsor integration between heavy and light industry, but the development of sophisticated intermediate industry is likely to be a more lengthy process than officials might anticipate.

The scope for new light industrial plant has been considerably widened by the government's conclusive moves against the private sector in 1980 and 1981. The forced closing of most retail outlets will also have knocked out a large proportion of

The Development of Libyan Industry

small industrial establishments, which were often no more than the back room of a shop.[37] It is government policy to consolidate light industry into larger units, and the introduction of new supermarket outlets is keeping the building industry active. The Secretariat of Light Industry has an Industrial Research Centre and limited statistical back-up to carry out feasibility studies.[38] Criticised at the 1981 People's Congress for lack of activity, the Secretariat has been busy in 1981 awarding turnkey contracts for dairies, animal feed factories, shoe manufacturing plants, bakeries, building-block factories, clothing factories, and olive oil processing plants. El Mehdawi's study of the manufacturing sector shows clearly that in the past light industry location has been determined by population location.[39] It is clear that a similar principle would still be advisable, although centralised planning may be obstructive in this respect. Some of the more modern and large scale industrial plants now operating or under construction are the $150 mn Cargi cigarette factory in Tripoli with 1,000 workers and a production capacity of 15-20 mn cigarettes an hour, a $104 mn textile complex at Beni Walid being built by West Germany, a $32 mn tyre factory at Tajurah, a flour mill near Tubruq with hourly capacity of 18,500 kilos, a plant for ready-to-wear suits in Darnah. A major achievement in 1981 was the completion of the country's first truck and bus construction plant. The suppliers, Iveco of Italy, put up 25 per cent of the capital of the plant and have promised to provide assistance to Libya's infant automotive component industry by supplying technology. A factory assembly operation is also in place at Tajurah and Libya is committed to buying a car plant, which will use more local components as they become available. Several industries are also planned in the plastics sector, including expansion of the Libyan-Norwegian Industrial Company's paint factory, and an extra 3 mn tons a year of cement capacity is due on stream imminently.[40]

CONCLUSION

Light industry seems likely to face an acute labour problem in the short term as other sectors are accorded greater priority. Many of the new factories are operating only one rather than two or three shifts. At present the accounting system for the light industrial sector is very lax. No charges are often made for utilities and there are incidents of wages being paid direct by the Secretariat. Light industry is unlikely to become a government priority unless foreign exchange availability is seriously curtailed, and so its expansion will tend to be modest with the largest growth area remaining building materials and bulk product sectors.

Summing up Libya's heavy industrial prospects, it seems fair to conclude that too much is being asked of this sector in a somewhat ill-defined way. There is a considerable need to press ahead with the planned projects both because Libya's capital surplus will not last for ever and because other gas producers may otherwise steal its position in the market. On the other hand the proposed pace of building will severely strain the country's human and physical infrastructure, and without a change of heart in marketing strategies will lead to a head-on clash with European protectionism. This, in turn, will only emphasise the contradiction inherent in the regime's expressed aim of self-sufficiency and import substitution for the economy as a whole and the self evident reliance of the heavy industrial sector, both in terms of its location and product mix, on the European market.

NOTES

1. McLachlan, K. S., 'Strategies for Agricultural Development in Libya'. See chapter 2.
2. El Mehdawi M., 'The Industrialisation of Libya', in *Change and Development in the Middle East* Methuen, London, 1981, pp 253-254
3. Sayigh, Y.A., *Economics of the Arab World* Croom Helm, London, 1978, pp 446-50
4. El Mehdawi, *op.cit.* pp 254-56
5. Ibid., pp 255-56
6. Sayigh, *op.cit.* p 460
7. Figures taken from Naur, M., 'The industrialisation Model of the Socialist People's Libyan Arab Jamahiriya', paper presented to conference on Economic and Social Development of Libya in the late Nineteenth and Twentieth Centuries, SOAS, University of London, 1981
8. *Middle East Economic Digest (MEED)*, 13 February 1981
9. El Mehdawi, *op. cit.* pp 262-63
10. *MEED*, 9 January 1981
11. *MEED*, 16 January 1981
12. Economist Intelligence Unit, *Oil in the Middle East - Annual Supplement*, 1980, p24

13. *MEED*, 4 September 1981
14. *MEED*, 28 August 1981; *MEED*, 24 October 1980; *Middle East Economic Survey (MEES)*, 14 September 1981
15. *8 Days*, 11 April 1981
16. *MEED*, 24 October 1980
17. *MEES*, 14 September 1981
18. *MEED*, 1 August 1980
19. *MEES*, 10 March 1980; *MEES*, 24 November 1980; *MEED*, 11 September 1981
20. Five Year Development Plan of Secretariat of Heavy Industry 1981-85 (in Arabic) and private communication with UK consultants.
21. *MEED*, 11 September 1981
22. *MEED*, 23 August 1981
23. *MEED* 23 January 1981
24. "Industrial Uses of Associated Gas in Oil Producing Developing Countries", *OAPEC Bulletin*, July 1980
25. Ibid.
26. Although an atomic Energy Secretariat was created in 1981, plans for an 800 mw power station in the Gulf of Surt seemed to have been shelved temporarily at least. Finland's state-owned power company Imatran-Voima, which was to have cooperated with the USSR in building the plant, had effectively abandoned these plans by September 1981. *MEED*, 9 October 1981
27. Libyan official concern at creating new urban growth poles through industry is discussed in Kezeiri, S.K., "Restructuring the urban system in Libya", paper presented to conference on Economic and Social Development in Libya, London, 1981
28. Speerplan GmbH and Finnmap Oy, *Al Khalij region - draft report of the regional plan, 1981-2000*, Secretariat of Municipalities, Tripoli, Chapter 8
29. *8 Days*, 5 September 1981
30. Naur, *op. cit.*
31. Details of Saudi petrochemical plans are synthesised in the *Third Five Year Plan, 1981-85*, Ministry of Planning, Riyadh
32. British Petroleum, *Our Industry Petroleum*, 1977, p 381
33. *MEES*, 31 December 1979
34. Barker, P., "Saudi Arabia's Twin Industrial Cities - Jubail and Yanbu", *Multinational Business*, No 1, 1981
35. *MEES*, 21 September 1981
36. *MEED*, 1 May 1981

The Development of Libyan Industry

37. 1981 saw the closure of privately owned textile, shoe and household appliance shops, as well as butchers and grocery stores (*MEED*, 27 March 1981). According to El Mehdawi light industrial production traditionally "was carried on chiefly in the bazaar, where retailing also took place" (p 253)

38. Consistent or comprehensive production figures for light industry are extremely difficult to obtain. Half year production figures in 1980 were announced as follows: milk products, 19 mn litres; flour, 110,000 tons; feedstuffs, 130,000 tons; aluminium piping, 5,200 tons; brick, 40,000 tones; shoes, 2012,306 pairs; skins, 1,960,000 sq ft; shoe leather, 84.5 tons; ready-to-wear men's suits, 152,000; macaroni, 55,380 tons; spun wool yarn, 360 tons; tinned foods, 18,420 tons; furniture, domestic and school, 65,250 tons, *Middle East Transport and Industry*, January/February 1981

39. El Mehdawi, *op. cit.*, pp 257-61

40. *Middle East Transport and Industry*, January/February 1981, and *MEED*, 21 August 1981, 9 October 1981

Chapter 6
THE LIBYAN FISHING INDUSTRY

E.W.Anderson & G.H.Blake

INTRODUCTION

With 1,685 km of coastline, and the second largest area of continental shelf in the Mediterranean (some 57,000 km^2 to 200 metres of water) Libya appears to have every opportunity for fishing. Libyan waters however are not particularly high in phytoplankton production, largely because of a shortage of nutrients. The north coasts of the Mediterranean are far more favourable for fish food production, but even these do not rank among the best fishing grounds in the world. With catches by non-Mediterranean States such as Japan taken into account, approximately 1.2 million tonnes of fish were caught in the Mediterranean and Black Sea in 1977 of which about three quarters was from the Mediterranean Sea. Total potential production from the Mediterranean is uncertain, but it seems clear that in some areas catches could be increased and this includes fishing grounds off Libya. Fish stocks are not unlimited, however, and optimum size of catch has been reached for several species already in the Mediterranean as a whole. At present Libya's fish catch is one of smallest in the Mediterranean (Table 1), but the Libyan government hopes to expand production to 8,000-12,000 tonnes by 1995.

HISTORICAL PERSPECTIVE

Pre-Italian period

There was very little indigenous fishing along the Libyan coast in the early years of the twentieth century. This relative neglect of fishing is surprising, but may be attributed to: coastal waters

The Libyan Fishing Industry

noted for frequent storms; lack of natural harbours; absence of a seafaring tradition and indifference to fish eating; ignorance about the productivity of coastal waters; high price of fish compared with meat; and a small and scattered population, many of whom favoured the hilly districts of the interior to the coast. The last point deserves emphasis; at the beginning of this century the population of Libya was probably around half a million, many of whom were nomads.

Table 1: Mediterranean and Black Sea fish catches by coastal states (1977) in tonnes

Albania	4,000	Libya	4,803+
Algeria	43,475	Malta	1,459
Bulgaria	10,172	Morocco	33,474
Cyprus	1,189	Romania	6,142
Egypt	6,683	Spain	140,957
France	44,011	Syria	826
Greece	71,842	Tunisia	38,441
Israel	3,600	Turkey	138,174
Italy	355,213	USSR	244,098
Lebanon	2,400	Yugoslavia	35,248

+FAO estimate: the 1977 catch was actually 2,475 tonnes

Source: *Yearbook of Fishery Statistics*, Vol 44, 1977, FAO 1978, Table C37

Details of fishing off Libya before the First World War are sketchy. A few small boats engaged in in-shore fishing, notably in Tripolitanian waters. Traditional sponge fishing was already highly developed, largely by the Greeks, and sponge production increased during the nineteenth century to reach an all-time peak of 71,883 kg in 1911. Foreign fishing boats (Greek, Maltese and Italian) also fished in Libyan waters and visited Libyan ports from time to time.

The Italian period 1911-1943

The Italians had some knowledge of Libyan waters, and appear to have been determined to exploit their potential for fish, sponges, corals and the cultivation of pearls. As early as 1912 fishing boats from Naples were sent to undertake fishing trials from

Tripoli, and in the same year a scientific survey of fisheries was attempted by Professor Scolart, with inconslusive results. A further survey was conducted in 1923, and, in 1923 and 1927, the Italian naval ship 'Tritone' carried out cruises in Libyan waters to collect data on sponge banks.[1] The Italian administration was clearly anxious to regulate and control the exploitation of offshore resources, particularly the sponge banks, and 'illegal' fishing was actively prevented. An interesting aspect of the use of the seabed in Italian times was the attempt from 1921 to cultivate pearls in Libyan coastal waters. The project never went beyond the experimental stage, though one report mentions 'harvesting' of pearls from the seabed in 1927. Both tuna fishing and sponge fishing reached their peak production during the inter-war period. The record year for sponges was 1929 (66,740 kg) and for tuna it was probably 1940 when 20,497 tuna were caught.[2] The number of tuna stations (or tonnara) in use during these years varied from 6 to 15.

Post-World War II to 1970

It is possible to put together a useful profile of Libyan fisheries during the post-war period because of FAO reports[3] and an International Bank survey of the economy of Libya.[4] Unfortunately, annual statistics of catches, apart from sponges, do not appear to have been systematically collected until the 1970s. Available figures tend to be ill-defined or unreliable, but it seems certain that total catches were in the 2,000 to 2,500 tonnes range through the 1950s, rising to 3,000 to 3,500 tonnes during the 1960s. In addition, foreign boats from Italy, Malta, and Greece fished in Libyan waters, marketing their catches at home. About half the Libyan catch was tuna, and a high proportion of the other half was sardines (*Sardinella aurita*) and anchovies (*Engraulis encrasicholus*). Two thirds of the catch was canned or salted for domestic consumption and export. The processing plants were generally poorly equipped, and confined to the Tripolitanian coast. These plants, particularly the tonnara, provided an important source of seasonal employment, the total labour force in the 1950s being over 1,000. The number of fishermen was probably around 200, including a number of foreigners resident in Libya. The annual value of the fish catch was put at £L 200,000

The Libyan Fishing Industry

- £L 250,000 and the sponge catch at £L 30,000 in 1958, or about 0.5 per cent of GNP. In general, fishing methods (other than sponge fishing) were regarded as rather primitive, the catch per man fishing day being as low as 10 kg, compared with 100 kg in many other Mediterranean countries.[5]

During the later years of this period, the sponge fishing industry virtually disappeared, while the number of tonnara in operation declined to five or six as a result of falling catches of tuna.

1970 - 1980

The 1970s witnessed significant advances in the Libyan fishing industry. Total catches rose to over 4,000 tonnes per annum, largely as a result of the operations of three companies using modern trawlers to exploit the waters of the continental shelf, beyond the range of traditional boats. Figures of catches for 1974-1979 show that Libyan catches doubled in about two decades, (Table 2).

Table 2. Libya: fish catches 1974-79 (in tonnes)

COMPANIES	1974	1975	1976	1977	1978	1979
Libya Fishing Company	308	173	366	229	200	120
Libya-Tunisia Company	351	659	293	310	430	312
Libya-Greece Company	-	-	-	-	-	464
Total	659	832	659	539	630	896
PRIVATE SECTOR						
Tripoli	2426	2722	1602	1022	1783	1676
Benghazi	280	312	317	316	1123	600
Zawia, Zuwarah	294	337	197	151	206	560
Al Khums, Misratah, Surt	325	506	1174	200	523	698
Darhah, Tobruq	343	96	111	247	90	70
Total	3668	3973	3401	1936	3725	3604
Grand Total	4327	4805	4060	2475	4355	4500

Source: Department of Production, Tripoli. September 1980

During the 1970s the government of Libya evolved plans to develop the fishing industry to its optimum level. Libya without oil is poorly endowed with natural resources, and diversification of the economy for the post-oil era is essential but costly. Fishing is an important part of the policy of diversification. Justification for embarking on massive investment in fisheries is based upon a number of reports by international consultants. While some of their proposals are probably over-optimistic, they provide important guidelines for government strategy.[6]

Under the Three Year Plan of 1973-75, improvement of the fishing ports at Al Khums, Tripoli and Zanzur was begun, and refrigeration facilities were constructed at Surt, Tubruq, Darnah, Susah, Ayn Ghazalah and Marsa Sabratah. Sardine canning factories with a capacity of 1,000 tonnes per annum were established at Zuwarah and Al Khums, and a 2,000 tonne capacity tuna plant was built at Zanzur. Other changes in the 1973-75 period are shown in Table 3. The Five Year Plan of 1976-80 took these projects further, and added a number of new features. Improvement of harbour facilities continued, and several new cold storage plants were established. The largest single project by far was the commencement of work on a major new port at Zuwarah. Several new joint companies were also founded to encourage fishing in deep waters. All these initiatives, together with investment in fisheries research and education were allocated large sums of money, which it is assumed have been largely spent (Table 4).

Table 3. Achievements of the 1973-75 Plan

	1973	1975
Libyan fish catch	2492 tonnes	4800 tonnes
Imported fish	4305 tonnes	4000 tonnes
Total consumption	6797 tonnes	8800 tonnes
Per capita consumption	3 kg	3.5 kg
Fishermen		
Libyan	300	500
Non-Libyan	200	300
Total fishermen	500	800

Source: Libyan Arab Republic, *The 1976-80 Socio-Economic Plan*, Ministry of Planning (1976), pp 233-255

Table 4. Budget Allocations for Fisheries 1976-80

Harbours, lighthouses, etc	LD 20,000,000
Expansion of companies	LD 5,000,000
Cooling and refrigeration plants	LD 10,851,000
Research and training	LD 2,500,000
Total	LD 38,351,000

Source: Libyan Arab Republic, *The 1976-80 Socio-Economic Plan*, Ministry of Planning (1976), p 243

Libya's determination to develop a modern fishing industry is further illustrated in the proposed budget allocations for the period 1981-85 (Table 5).

Table 5. Budget allocations for fisheries 1981-85

	Total for 1981-85	Allocated for 1981
Research	LD 2,500,000	LD 1,000,000
Equipment and services	LD 92,995,000	LD 19,105,000
Company ventures etc	LD 62,000,000	LD 34,000,000
Training	LD 20,000,000	LD 5,000,000
Education	LD 1,000,000	LD 400,000
Salaries and consultancy	LD 1,500,000	LD 290,000
Total	LD 179,995,000	LD 59,795,000

Source: Secretary for Light Industries, *Programme for Development of Marine Resources, 1981-85*, February 1980, p 77

MARINE PRODUCTIVITY

The productivity of Libya's coastal waters is an important question, since this imposes the ultimate constraint on the size of catch, regardless of the level of investment. Commercial fisheries are normally concerned with the third stage of the food chain. The initial two stages, primary and secondary production, are therefore vital and need to be considered. In each it is necessary to measure the quantity of production, the geographical distribution and, crucially, variations of both in time. Such research requires long-term investigations particularly as the relationship between fisheries and plankton, especially in the case of demersal fish, is complex. Results of the main research programme completed in the waters off Tripolitania are detailed in the Sogreah Report (1975).[7] However, it must be stressed that the research involved an incomplete sampling procedure over only two seasons.

According to the Sogreah maps showing primary production for spring and summer there is a definite increase in productivity westwards. Possible reasons for this include:

1. The generally shallow nature of the water allowing more light and higher temperatures at the lowest levels;
2. The dense banks of weed which commonly occur and provide a suitable ecological milieu for plankton development;
3. The contribution of nutrient salts by the *ghibli*, the strong southerly dust bearing wind.

Secondary production, zooplankton, provides an essential link between primary production and the upper levels of the food chain. Again the maps suggest an increase in productivity westwards. Thus productivity in the first two stages of the food chain shows a definite increase westwards along the Tripolitanian coast and into Tunisian waters where the maximum levels are recorded. In general, primary and secondary productivity decline towards the east so that fishing prospects in the Gulf of Surt and off Cyrenaica are not very great, though the CONTRANSIMEX and INSTRUPA reports indicate local opportunities (see 6c and 6d).

TYPES OF FISHING

A considerable variety of fishing methods can be found in Libyan waters, reflecting in part skills inherited from foreign fishermen, as well as indigenous techniques.

1. Inshore fishing

Small boats of less than eight metres operate from approximately 30 locations along the coast of Libya to a maximum distance of 5 or 6 nautical miles offshore. Most are motorised, and their crews are either full-time or part-time Libyan fishermen. Several techniques are used:

Nets: gill nets and trammel nets are used at depths of 35 to 40 metres.
Lines of between 1,500 and 4,000 metres in length may be used at depths of up to 80 metres.
Fixed lines (or brinkali) are commonly used in up to 40 metres of water. Lines of up to 1,500 metres are put out using float and sinker. These may remain in position for 12 hours or more. In summer 1980 the average number of *brinkali* in place in Tripolitania was reported as follows: Zuwarah 20, Tripoli 30; Al Khums 10; Kliten 10; Misratah 20. *Brinkali* may be found as far as six nautical miles offshore in certain coastal waters.

The chief species of fish commonly landed by inshore fishermen are as follows:

Galeorhinus galeus (dog-fish)
Epinephalus guaza (dusky perch)
Dentex vulgaris (sea bream)
Polyprion americanum (stone bass)
Mustelus mustelus (smoth hound)
Umbrina cirrhosa (corb)
Squantina squantina (monkfish)
Diplodus sargus (a sea bream)
Diplodus vulgaris (a sea bream)
Lithognatus mormyrus (a sea bream)
Deplodus annularis (a sea bream)
Oblada melanura (saddled bream)

The list of typical species is far from complete. The variety of fish in Libyan waters is remarkable. Several types of crustaceans, molluscs, and other bottom dwellers, are caught from time to time and sold in the fish markets. It would be misleading to claim that they are a speciality of Libyan waters, but their regular appearance in the markets is evidence of Libyan exploitation of species living primarily on the continental shelf. Some examples are as follows:

Lobsters, prawn, etc:
Parapenaeus longiroitris
Plesiopenaeus edwardsianus
Homarus gammarus (lobster)
Palaemon serratus (prawn)

Crabs and crayfish:
Scyllarides latus
Palinurus vulgaris (crayfish)
Maja squinado (spiny spider crab)
Squids and octopuses:
Loligo vulgaris (common squid)
Sepiola rondeleti
Octopus vulgaris (common octopus)

2. Lampara fishing

Fishing for sardines and anchovies is done in summer between May and October, at night, the best catches being in July and August. Boats of between 7 and 13 metres work in pairs, one boat carrying a lamp to attract the fish. Surface seine nets are used, with small sinkers. Most lampara fishing is within six nautical miles of the shore. During autumn and winter some lampara boats fish for bonito and mackerel. The chief species landed by lampara fishermen are:

Sardinella aurita (sardine)
Engraulis encrasicholus (anchovy)
Trachurus trachurus (horse-mackerel)
Auxis thazard (frigate mackerel)

3. Trawler fishing in Libyan waters

Small trawlers of 16 to 27 metres fish largely within 12 nautical miles of the Libyan coast, and always within the continental shelf. There is little trawling in summer. Three companies were active in 1980/81, with 22 trawlers in operation. The Libyan Fishing Company (seven trawlers) was founded in 1970, the Libya-Tunisia Company in 1972 (four trawlers), and the Libya-Greece Company in 1978 (eleven trawlers). All three companies also own a number of smaller fishing boats. In addition, one or two groups of fishermen owned and operated small trawlers. There are plans to expand the number of trawlers operating in Libyan waters very rapidly, to a total of 95 in 1985, with a combined potential catch of over 9,000 tonnes.[8] This target is thought to be too high, particularly in the light of manpower shortages. The chief species of fish caught by trawlermen are:

Mullus barbatus (red mullet)
Mullus surmeletus (striped mullet)
Pagellus erythrinus (pandora)
Merluccius merluccius (hake)
Trachurus trachurus (horse mackerel)
Pagellus centrodentus (Spanish bream)
Maena maena
Balistes carolinensis (trigger fish)
Boops boops (bogue)
Boops salpa (saupe)
Squatina squatina (monkfish)
Mustelus mustelus (smooth hound)

4. Tuna fishing

Fishing for tuna has been practised along the Tripolitanian coast for several decades. The method depends on the useof a heavy 'leader' net anchored firmly to the seabed and suspended from huge floats, extending seawards to a depth of about 45 metres. A large trap net to catch the tuna is similarly anchored to the seabed at the seaward end of the leader net. The migrating tuna moving along the coast from west to east are trapped as they try to evade the leader net. They are then lifted into boats and brought ashore for salting or canning. Tuna can weigh up to 500 kg and the whole installation (known as 'tonnara') requires 100 tonnes of rope and net and a large quantity of heavy anchors and floats. Although the season lasts only about 40 days (mostly in June, depending on location), it takes three months to prepare the nets and anchor them to the seabed. Thus for several months the tonnara constitute a hazard to shipping, extending from two to three nautical miles offshore. Warnings to shipping are placed farther out to sea, and the tonnara are noted in various pilots' handbooks.[9]

The number of tonnara has declined from a peak of 15 before the Second World War to four in 1980. Over 60 men are required to man the tuna nets of one tonnara during the catching season, and perhaps 250 more will be employed for two months to process the tuna. Most of the temporary employees are local farmers for whom the tuna season is a welcome bonus. Clearly the cost of operating a tonnara is high, and unless a heavy crop of tuna is obtained, it is easy to lose money. Tuna catches have declined in Libya and elsewhere in the Mediterranean in recent years. Pollution, and changing migration patterns have been blamed, but the most likely explanation is the increasing exploitation of the Atlantic tuna population. Tuna caught off Libya are largely Atlantic Red Tuna (Thunnus thynnus) heading for spawning grounds in the east-central Mediterranean. The extent to which catches have declined in Libya is difficult to assess since the only statistics available are incomplete and ambiguous. Figures for the period 1951-1964 indicate an overall decline, though it has to be remembered that fluctuations occur as a result of storms, and the number of tonnara in operation. The figures in Table 6 may be compared with 499 tonnes (3880 tuna) in 1971 and 236 tonnes in 1972. The number of tuna caught in 1980 was reported to be: Zliten 1,000; Misratah 2,000; Garabulli 400; Sabratah 400. If the average fish size was the same in 1980 as in 1971, the 1980 catch would be 617 tonnes.

Table 6. Catches of tuna (in tonnes) 1951-1964

1951	1149	1956	1399	1961	145
1952	1004	1957	1800	1962	866
1953	1785	1958	1154	1963	529
1954	833	1959	1246	1964	293
1955	791	1960	734		

Source: Sogreah, *Study for a General Master Plan for the Development of the Fishing in the Libyan Arab Republic*, Part 1, Grenoble, 1973, p 39

Tuna fishing in Libya is unlikely to expand or contract greatly in the next few years. Its contribution to Libya's economy is not great, but it should be remembered that the tuna industry was important when Libya was among the poorest countries in the world. The tonnara (including the processing plants) employed between 1,500 and 2,000 in the tuna season, and with sardines contributed approximately 10 per cent of the total value of Libya's exports.[10]

5. Deep-sea fishing

A number of joint fishing companies were established in the 1970s between Libya and foreign partners to fish in distant waters. Seven such companies were in existence in 1981 and others were under negotia-

The Libyan Fishing Industry

tion. Those in existence were: Libya-Malta, Libya-Mauritania, Libya-Benin. Libya-Guinea, Libya-Spain, Libya-South Yemen, and Libya-Guiana. The Libyan fishing industry was thus acquiring valuable experience and knowledge of deep-sea fisheries.

6. Sponge fishing

Table 7 summarises sponge catches landed in Libya by local boats only, between 1920 and 1962. Since 1962 the decline continued, and in 1980 only two sponge boats were operating in Libya. In the period 1920-1960 approximately 100 to 200 sponge boats of various kinds fished in Libyan waters annually, about 10 per cent being Libyan boats. The decline is largely due to competition with cheap sponge substitutes, and the dangers associated with sponge diving. Sponge production fluctuated from year to year, total yields from Libyan waters ranging between 30 and 140 tonnes a year, the average being around 80 tonnes from 1900 to 1960. A considerable proportion of total production was by foreign boats, chiefly Greek. Table 8 shows total production compared with local Libyan production from 1948 to 1951.

Table 7. Sponges landed in Libya by local boats 1920-1962

(kg)

Year	kg	Year	kg	Year	kg
1920	47,108	1931	36,559	1953	14,695
1921	18,091	1932	47,424	1954	21,103
1922	20,425	1933	25,947	1955	32,520
1923	24,779	1934	30,972	1956	20,315
1924	16,919	1935-46	N/A	1957	21,007
1925	19,789	1947	20,195	1958	6,990
1926	49,750	1948	29,994	1959	15,341
1927	40,250	1949	8,439	1960	2,671
1928	46,400	1950	25,000	1961	19,101
1929	66,740	1951	34,954	1962	3,885
1930	N/A	1952	30,781		

Source: Kingdom of Libya, *Statistical Abstract 1963*, Ministry of National Economy, Tripoli, 1964, p 165

Although Libyan sponge banks were intensively fished for generations, they showed no signs of exhaustion. The FAO report attributes this to the vast area of Libyan sponge grounds, estimated to be around 15,000 square kilometres[11] nearly all in depths of less than 120 metres. Scarcely a stretch of Libyan coast has not been fished for sponges in the past, and some rich sponge banks have also been worked at great distances from the coast. The following, for example, were specified by Serbetis in the FAO report of 1952:[12]

1. The Lapsi bank 83 miles north-north-east of Zuwarah;
2. The Trafili bank 17 miles east of the Lapsi bank;
3. The Fondazzo bank 75 miles north of Zuwarah;
4. The Foro bank 22 miles north-north-east of Ras Makaber.

The best survey of sponge fishing was incorporated into the FAO report of 1952, and this remains a standard source of scientific and historic detail on the subject.

Table 8. Sponge production by local boats and total production from Libyan waters 1948-51

Year	Total production (1) (kg)	Landed by local boats (2)
1947	138,665	20,195
1948	75,036	29,994
1949	98,887	8,439
1950	120,000	25,000
1951	100,723	34,954

Source: (1) C D Serbetis, *Report to the Government of Libya on the Fisheries of Libya*, FAO Rome, 1952, p 37
(2) Kingdom of Libya, *Statistical Abstract 1963*, Ministry of National Economy, Tripoli, 1974, p 165

Methods of sponge fishing

1. Primitive diving in shallow waters (20-30 metres) without equipment; this method had become very rare by 1950.

2. Waterglass and sponge hook
   Having located sponges through a waterglass, they were removed using a harpoon which could be used with skill, in up to 25

metres of water

3. Machine diving
   The diver wore a rubber suit and received air pumped through a rubber pipe.

4. Fernez diving
   The method in which a rubber mask is used in lieu of the diving suit. A rubber pipe supplies air to the diver.

5. Gangava system
   A dredge of two by five metres was dragged over the sponge bank by a motor-powered vessel. Sponges obtained were usually abundant, but of poor quality.

Since 1900, approximately two thirds of sponge production has been from divers using rubber suits or the Fernez system. In 1950 for example, 81 boats (chiefly Greek) operated divers, and 52 boats used other methods.

NUMBER OF BOATS

The estimated number of fishing boats using certain ports in Libya in 1979 is given in Table 9. It will be noted that they were distributed throughout the Libyan coast, with a marked concentration towards the west where the population is greatest and fisheries most productive. The total number of boats was 338, excluding specialised boats associated with tuna fishing. About 90 per cent were motor-powered boats. The figures in Table 9, however, do not correspond with a survey conducted in 1972-73 which counted 467 boats, including 180 in Tripoli.[13] If tuna boats are excluded, the total is still over 400. It is unlikely that numbers had fallen since 1973; fish catches had increased, and the number of fishermen rose from 500 to 800 from 1972-75. The discrepancy probably lies in differences of definition or data collection, the higher figure being more acceptable. Several boats of traditional wooden build were seen to be under construction in September 1980, and there was every sign that the fishing boat fleet would grow in the coming decade. In the 1972-73 survey, 78 per cent of boats were under 8 metres in length.

Table 9. Fishing boats in Libya 1979

Port	Trawlers	Small and medium size boats	Total capacity (tonnes)
Bu Kammash	-	20	300
Marsa Zuwarah	-	24	600
Tripoli	8	120	2450
Al Khums	-	45	500
Zoruq (Misratah)	-	12	300
Surt	-	12	300
Benghazi	5	45	3500
Tulmaythah	-	12	300
Susah	-	15	300
Ayn Ghazalah	-	20	400
Total	13	325	8950

Source: Secretary for Light Industry, *Programme for Development of Marine Resources*, 1981-83, Tripoli, 1980, p 67

NUMBER OF FISHERMEN

Sogreah gave the following details, which are assumed to refer to 1973 (Table 10). Accurate figures are again difficult to obtain, partly because part-time fishermen are still common among inshore fishermen in Libya. It is also worth noting that recreational fishing was becoming more popular. The number of professional fishermen in 1981 was estimated to be between 1,000 and 1,200.

Table 10. Number of fishermen by region

Region	Total fishermen	Of which foreigners
Zuwarah	151	32
Tripoli	420-470	200-250
Al Khums	46	15
Misratah	100	20
Benghazi	90	40
Al Bayda	10	-
Darnah	55	41
Total	872-922	348-398

Source: Sogreah, *Study for a General Master Plan for the Development of the Fishing Ports in the Libyan Arab Republic*, Part 1, Grenoble, 1973, p 25

The Libyan Fishing Industry

FUTURE EXPANSION OF LIBYAN FISHING

Sogreah made a useful estimate of the potential for expanding Libyan fisheries in 1973, though their conclusions were extremely optimistic. It is important to realise however that recommendations of Sogreah and other consultants have been used as guidelines for the large investment now taking place in Libyan fisheries, the results of which were already tangible by 1981. Table 11 gives an idea of the scale of expansion proposed by Sogreah.

Table 11. Proposals for the expansion of Libyan fishing

	Slow growth (3%)		Rapid growth (5%)	
	1990	1995	1990	1995
INSHORE FISHING				
Boats	564	656	772	983
Catch in tonnes	6272	8150	8580	12280
TRAWLING	1985	1990		
Trawlers	55	77		
Catch in tonnes	8195	13500		

SPONGE FISHING

Catches of 3,000 to 5,000 kg per annum from 32 teams working from 70 boats

MANPOWER REQUIREMENTS	1985	1990
Captains and mates:		
trawlers, etc	182	186
lamparas, inshore boats, etc	750	850
Mechanics	518	553
Sailor fishermen and divers	4455	4730
Total	5905	6319

Source: Sogreah, *Study for a General Master Plan for the Development of the Fishing Ports in the Libyan Arab Republic*, Part II Grenoble, 1973, pp 42-53

While Commercial fisheries in Libya could certainly be expanded considerably, it is doubtful whether such targets can be achieved, certainly in the period to 1990. The Libyan government is however clearly committed to a policy of fisheries expansion: probably the most spectacular evidence is the new port at Zuwarah. The new fisheries complex

at Zuwarah will be the most modern in the
Mediterranean and, for its size, probably one of the
most efficient in the world. The harbour has 470
metres of quays for larger trawlers and 220 metres
for smaller vessels. There are spacious fish handling facilities linked to a 1,000 tonne freezing
plant capable of producing 30 tonnes of ice per day.
Near by are two large maintenance blocks to facilitate net mending, a general store and a gear store
in which each ship will be allocated its own compart-
ment. There is also a large ship repair area,
capable of handling 450 tonne trawlers, and a range
of services for the fishermen, including a medical
and residential centre. With its own generator and
power plant, the whole complex will be virtually
self-sufficient. Such large-scale investment
reflects Libyan confidence in the development of its
fisheries within and beyond home waters.

Notes

1. Mazarelli, G., 'La pesca sui banchi di spugne esplorat: con la R. N. 'Tritone', *Soc. Italiana Per II Progresse Delle Science*, November 1936, pp 4-15
2. Kingdom of Libya, *Statistical Abstract 1963*, Ministry of National Economy, Tripoli, 1964 p 164 and see Serbetis, C.D. (1952) p 52
3. Serbetis, C. D., *The Present situation of Libyan fisheries*, FAO Report No 187, Rome, 1958
4. International Bank for Reconstruction and Development, *The Economic Development of Libya*, Johns Hopkins Press, Baltimore, 1960
5. International Bank (1960), p 204
6. The relevant reports are:
(a) Sogreah (consulting engineers), *Study for a general masterplan for the development of the fish-ing ports in the Libyan Arab Republic*, Final report, April 1975 - Part 1 - Present situation, August 1973: Part 2 - General development plan of fishing activities, December 1973: Part 3 - Preliminary general masterplan, August 1974. In collaboration with Ministry of Industry and Minerals, Department of Aquatic Wealth, Sogreah, Grenoble, France, 1973. (Sogreah recommended exploitation of available fish resources to the optimum by 1985, with special ref-erence to harbour facilities).
(b) Sogreah, *Trawl fishing ground survey off the Tripolitanian coast*, Part 1 - Bathymetry and sediment-ology: Part 2 - Hydrology: Part 3 - Nutrient salts and primary production: Part 4 - Secondary produc-tion: Part 5 - Fishery biology and trawling

resources study. Final report: Introduction and general conclusions, August 1977. In collaboration with Ministry of Food and Wealth, General Department of Marine Wealth, Sogreah, Grenoble, France, 1977. (Sogreah began this work in 1973, but the scientific findings were of limited value; the report recommended the optimisation of fish production in a favourable marine environment)
(c) Contransimex (Rumania) *Oceanographic survey in the eastern territorial waters of the Libyan Arab Republic between Ras Azzaz and Ras Kar Kura, May 1975 - August 1976* Two volumes, 1977
(Contransimex reported that demersal stocks (bottom communities) are underexploited, though they are not abundant. Medium-size trawlers could be introduced to supply the local market).
(d) Instrupa (West Germany) *Final report on results of the test fishing program, Gulf of Surt, Libyan Arab Republic,*Tannenwaldallec, F R Germany, July 1975
(The prospects for commercial fisheries in the Gulf of Surt were found to be quite good. Shrimps could be very abundant).

    7.   Sogreah (1975), Vols 1-5
    8.   Secretary for Light Industry, *Plan for development of marine resources 1981-85*, Tripoli, February 1980, p 63
    9.   See for example, Hydrographer of the Navy, *Mediterranean Pilot*, Vol V, 6th edition, Taunton, England, 1976, p 39, which warns that tonnara may extend five miles offshore.
    10.   Serbetis, C.D., (1952), p 52
    11.   Serbetis, C.D., (1952), pp 39-40
    12.   Serbetis, C.D., (1952), p 7
    13.   Sogreah (1973), Vol 1, p 23

The Libyan Fishing Industry

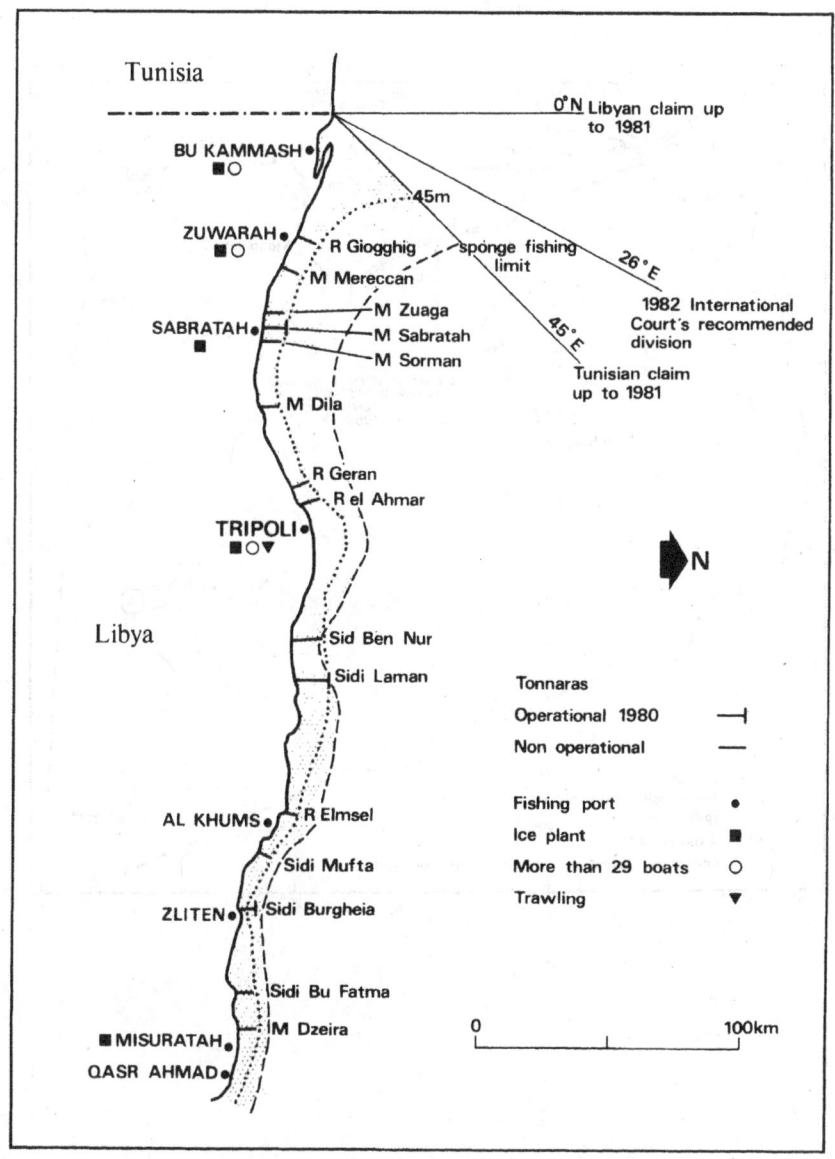

Figure 5 Western Libya, Fishing Ports, Tonnaras, and Sponge Limits

Transport and Investment

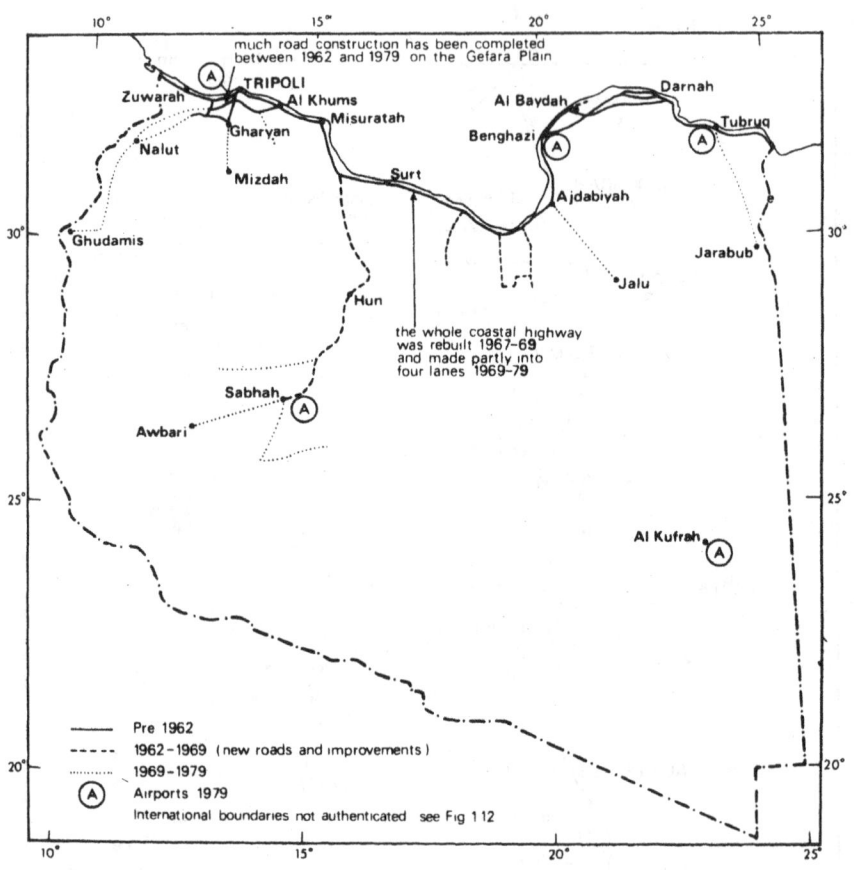

Figure 6   Libya's Road Network 1950-1979

Chapter 7
TRANSPORT AND INVESTMENT IN THE LIBYAN JAMAHIRIYA 1963-1980

Abulgasim M. Elazzabi

INTRODUCTION

Because of the importance of the transport sector in the country's economy, Libyan policy makers have paid this sector significant attention since the mid-sixties and the development of transportation has played an essential role in connecting the elements of the economy. Many Third World countries tend to spend a high proportion of their development investment in extending and improving the infrastructure of transport. In developed countries the share of the transport sector in GDP varies between 10 and 15 percent, while its share in the developing countries differs considerably from one country to another according to the basic activities of the economy and the level of industrialisation. For example, in Chad, transport's share of the GDP was 17 percent while in Zambia which produces high value minerals, transport accounted for only 7 percent of GDP.[1] In the Jamahiriya where oil has been the main source of income, transport hardly accounted for 5 percent of GDP in 1975 and 1980. Transport had meanwhile attracted a high proportion of investment (more than 12 percent of total investment). There are special circumstances however brought about by the effect of oil on the economy.[2]

In Libya oil revenues transformed the economy and affected the style and the extent of the development of transport. Governments with large oil revenues to dispose approach the provision of roads and related transport facilities differently from those operating on restricted budgets. In addition the expectations of the people participating in the fruits of an oil economy are high and these high expectations extend to the type of road network to be made available as well as the width and quality of the carriageways. Road transport has been given a great deal of attention in all of Libya's development plans.

THE NEED FOR INVESTMENT ON TRANSPORT

Before oil Libya was one of the poorest countries in the world with agriculture its main economic activity. Agriculture was and has remained a precarious activity in Libya's marginal environment and thus at independence per capita income was as low as Libyan dinars (LD) 14 per annum.[3] The first decade of independence was a period of economic dependence on foreign aid and allocations to road transport up to 1963 were modest.[4]

With oil revenues the economic indicators such as GDP and income per head rose substantially. Between 1962 and 1968 national income rose from LD 146.6 mn to LD 558.9 mn and GDP (at factor cost) from LD 177.2 to LD 835.3 at current prices. Population was rising rapidly in the same period from 1.455 millions to 1.808 millions but national income per head rose from LD 100.8 to LD 309.0 at constant 1964 prices.[5] The period saw the first development plan, 1963-1968, with allocations to production and services sectors. Transport was amongst the sectors to attract investment and as a result of the schemes initiated by the plan 868 kilometres of road were constructed by 1968 and 3400 were in the process of construction, including the coastal highway (1769 kilometres). Other transport facilities were improved such as the handling capacities of the ports of Tripoli and Benghazi. New storage areas and quays were constructed and modern equipment for handling cargo was installed. Airports were also improved, new runways constructed, and new aircraft acquired.

A World Bank study[6] emphasised that "transport is a necessary commitment of the exchange economy and it is indispensible to economic growth". The developments in the early years of oil revenues indicate that in matters of road transport, the ports and air transport, changes were being planned and effected which were consistent with a reduction of travel times and the promotion of economic activity. At the same time it was confirmed that improved transportation systems cannot by themselves create development. Effective resource utilisation and economic activity require a balanced investment policy with attention being given to the provision of an

Transport and investment

adequate overall economic and social infrastructure.

INVESTMENT BETWEEN 1963 and 1980

The development of transportation in the period 1963-1980 has been effected in a climate of almost constantly improving national revenues. The period can be divided into four according to the phases defined by the various planning agencies which drew up investment plans. The first period was that of the first five year plan (1963-1968), the second has been termed the transition period 1969-1972, the third was that of the three year development plan 1973-1975, and finally the development plan of 1976-1980.

The First Five Year Development Plan 1963-1968

The 1963-1968 plan was the first of its kind since the 1930s and it was drawn up in response to the promise of oil revenues. These did in the event increase between 1962 and 1968 at a rate of 105 per cent per year, from LD 7 mn in 1962 to 280 mn in 1968.[7] Allocations to development totalled LD 337 mn (current prices) out of which LD 71 mn (21.1 per cent) was to go to transport, placing transport second in importance after public works (24.4 per cent). According to national accounts published in 1980, the LD 71 mn allocated to transport was not spent and only LD 53 mn was in fact expended, representing 17.8 per cent of total development spending.[8] A reason for the shortfall was the difficulty of mobilising investment before the appropriate studies had been carried out, and it was not until the mid 1960s that a comprehensive study was completed by the consultants, Doxiadis.

In addition to the improvements in the road network already mentioned, and the port improvements at Tripoli and Benghazi, the small ports of Darnah and Tubruq attracted some investment and the passenger handling capacity of the airports increased from 146,000 in 1963 to 500,000 in 1967.[9]

The Transitional Period 1969-1972

The first of September Revolution in 1969 brought to power a group with new ideas and a sense of urgency in promoting their implementation. Because

Transport and investment

economic development can only be achieved gradually the ambitious policies outlined initially were modified. Nevertheless there was a substantial increased in the allocations to transport and in the expenditures achieved. For example in the 1971-1973 period LD 113 mn were allocated and LD 76 mn were expended. Table 1 shows the comparision between the rates of allocation and expenditure for the first five year plan period and the post-revolutionary period 1971-1973. Although the budgeted targets were not reached, actual spending in the 1971-1973 period ran at a rate four times that achieved in the earlier period at current prices.

Table 1: Comparision of allocation and expenditure on transport between 1963-1968 and 1971-1977

Period	Allocation LD mn	Expenditure LD mn	Yearly average LD mn
1963-1968	71.2	51.7	10.3
1971-1973	112.9	75.8	37.9

Source: Secretariat of Planning, 1980, *The National Accounts* 1971-1978, Tripoli

Investment in transport was promoted vigorously after the revolution in order to provide an appropriate infrastructure for the expansion of the productive sectors of agriculture and industry.

The Three Year Development Plan 1973-1975

The major developments of transport systems of the Jamahiriya was initiated with the 1973-1975 development plan. It was very clear in the early 1970s that the nation's harbours were unable to cope with the increasing volume of imports, and the road network, with the exception of the coastal highway was inadequate for the growing passenger and commercial traffic.

Table 2 indicates the massive increase in all types of development spending. Transport allocations were more than sevenfold those of 1963-1968 at current prices, and were more than double the total development allocations of the 1963-1968 plan. The average annual allocation was LD 128 mn, a high figure even taking into account inflation and a very high figure in terms of the absorptive capacity of the economy.

Table 2: Three year development plan allocation and expenditure 1973-1975   LD mn at current prices

Sector	Expenditure	Yearly average	Percentage of expenditure
Agriculture	436.2	145.4	16.4
Oil and mining	84.7	28.2	3.2
Manufacturing	324.5	108.1	12.2
Electricity and gas	325.5	108.5	12.2
Construction	82.0	24.0	3.1
Trade and insurance	21.9	7.3	0.8
Communications and storage	382.9	127.6	14.4
Housing	592.6	197.5	22.3
Education and health	236.8	78.9	8.9
Other services	174.7	58.2	6.5
Total	2164.4	887.4	100.0

Source: Secretariat of Planning, 1976, *Evaluation of the Three Year Development Plan*, Tripoli

Transport allocations though larger in absolute terms were smaller than before with respect to other sectors. Only 14.4 per cent of total development spending was allocated to communications and storage. This reduction did not reflect a reduction in the importance of transport so much as an increase in the emphasis given to the productive sectors of agriculture and industry and a continuing emphasis on housing. Within the transport sector itself great emphasis was given to harbours and sea transport with these receiving 47.8 per cent of the allocations. Roads and road transport were to receive 21.5 per cent of the total transport investment: telecommunications were to receive 7.8 per cent of the spending followed in fourth place by aviation.

The Five Year Development Plan 1976-1980

Recognising the need for a more comprehensive policy for national and regional development[10] a longer

Transport and investment

term plan was formulated for the period 1976-1980. The improvement of transport facilities was amongst the goals of those who devised the plan. The scale of investment was again to be increased and it was estimated that LD 7,600 mn would be spent on development. Total annual spending was expected to run at LD 1520 mn compared with LD 734 mn for 1973-1975. The allocations proved to be more than adequate as some sectors did not achieve the expenditures proposed.[11]

The transport sector continued to occupy third place, after industry and agriculture, but with a further reduction in the proportion of total at 12.6 per cent of proposed spending. At LD 960 mn per year transport spending was nevertheless to be 50 per cent greater than in the previous plan period, reflecting an increase in the number of projects proposed and the effects of inflation.

Table 3: Development of the transport sector - 1975-1980

Sub-sector				Change %
Paved roads	Km	7747.0	10,700.0	38.1
Cars per kilometre	No	37.8	62.2	64.5
Civil plans	No	10.0	17.0	70.0
Air passengers	No ('000)	559.0	1,125.0	100.1
Commercial ships	Ton ('000)	18.3	39.3	114.0
Oil tankers	Ton ('000)	412.0	766.0	86.0
Ports capacity	Mn ton	3.0	7.0	133.3
Telephone/person	No	1.8	6.0	290.0

Source: Secretariat of Planning,1980, *The Evaluation of the Five Year Development Plan,* Tripoli

The investment of the 1976-1980 period brought substantial improvements in the nation's communications. Most dramatic were the improvements in telecommunications. Sea trasnport responded to the investments and there was steady improvement in the road network.

OIL REVENUES AND TRENDS IN TRANSPORT INVESTMENT

By whatever means an analysis be carried out a close relationship will be shown between the level of oil

Transport and investment

revenues and levels of investment in the various sectors of the economy. Such patterns are common in oil economies, as is the condition that the transport sector contributes a small proportion of the GDP, 4.8 per cent in 1975 and 1978 (see Table 4).

Table 4: Gross Domestic Product for 1975 and 1980

Sector	1975 LDmn	1980 LDmn	Percentage %	%
Agriculture	82.9	99.0	2.2	1.9
Petroleum	1961.1	2236.0	53.4	44.2
Industry	103.8	245.0	2.8	4.8
Construction	434.7	579.0	11.8	11.4
Transport	175.8	245.0	4.8	4.8
Services	917.0	1654.0	25.0	32.9
Total	3674.3	5058.0	100.0	100.0

Source: Secretariat of Planning, 1980, *The Evaluation of the Five Year Development Plan*, Tripoli

It is not only in the transport sector that oil revenues play an important role. They have also been the basis of the other sectors of the economy. Table 4 shows that the services sector made the greatest quantitative improvement in the 1975-1980 period. The role of transport in making possible such growth is just as important for the services sector as for the productive sectors. Transport will play an essential role in sustaining the level of construction, the proposed growth in agricultural and industrial production as well as further developments in the services sector. Meanwhile the servicing of the high levels of investment needed to promote the integrated development of the economy will have to come from the success of such integrated economic development, as the pattern of oil revenues so closely correlated with the level of transport investment will continue to decline in relative terms.

Notes

1. World Bank, 1972, *Transportation: Sector Working Paper*, Washington DC, pp 3-4
2. Secretariat of Planning, 1980 (December) *The Evaluation of the Five Year Development Plan*, Tripoli

Transport and investment

3. Corporation of Planning, 1971, *Document Number Three*, Tripoli, p 2
4. IBRD, 1960, *The Economic Development of Libya*, Report of a mission organised by the IBRD, Johns Hopkins Press, Baltimore
5. Ministry of Planning, 1972, *National Accounts 1962-1971*, Tripoli
6. World Bank, 1972, *op. cit.*
7. Secretariat of Petroleum, 1972, *Libyan Oil 1954-1971*, Tripoli, p 131
8. Secretariat of Planning, 1980, *National Accounts 1971-1978*, Tripoli
9. Corporation of Planning, 1971, *op.cit.*
10. Hoyle, B.S. (editor) 1973, *Transport and Development: Geographical Readings*, pp 9-17
11. Secretariat of Planning, 1980, *op.cit.*
12. Secretariat of Planning, 1980 (January) *The Five Year Development Plan*, 1981-1985, Tripoli

PART 2

ASPECTS OF SOCIAL AND POLITICAL DEVELOPMENT

Chapter 8
CULTURAL AND SOCIAL DIVERSITY IN LIBYA

E.L. Peters

When the three provinces of Tripolitania, Fezzan and Cyrenaica were amalgamated to form the State of Libya on 24 December 1951, it included three territories which were economically, historically, culturally, and in their social organisation, quite disparate. The ethnic composition in each also differed significantly. As late as the period preceding independence, the divergence of interests in the three territories was made evident during the discussions in the National Assembly at which the members of each, with their divergent interests uppermost in their minds, failed to agree on any fundamental issue, although they were cajoled into compromise on most of them. The fact that the State was founded on a federal basis, in the first place, is further testimony of the deep divisions that had long existed, and the constitutional recognition given to the twin capitals of Tripoli and Benghazi reflected the severance of the two most populated territories by the inhospitably arid Gulf of Surt hinterland, where the desert comes down to the sea. The contemporary official stress that is given to the unitary nature of the State has yet to expunge the cultural cleavages of which the three territories were symptomatic, and which are deeply rooted in history.
    Discounting the pockets of minority populations, like the Jews (who, in some areas were highly concentrated, in al Qassabat for example, where the Jewish olive farmers constituted the majority of the village population), the Greeks, and the even smaller pockets of other European nationals, several ethnic groups have long been present in the population in significant numbers: Turks in the towns, Berbers in western Tripolitania, Tuareg and

Tebu inhabiting the interior oases, ex-slaves, mainly from the Sudan in Cyrenaica and from West Africa in Tripolitania, scattered throughout the country; and of course, people of Arab origin are distributed widespread. Six ethnic categories are still present in Libya, and most of the language distinctions, which characterised them in the past, still persist. Also, it is possible that a certain degree of occupational specialisation, related to ethnic origin, is beginning to appear, although the grounds for supposing this to be occurring, in the absence of careful research on the matter, are somewhat impressionistic. The kind of thing I have in mind is the number of Tebu engaged in menial tasks, and who live among the ruins in the old town of al-Marj. The same tendency is to be seen in the number of Egyptians employed in service trades in the towns, and as shepherds, herdsmen and cultivators in the countryside. Previously teaching, both in schools and the universities, was almost exclusively in Egyptian hands. By now, Libya has produced sufficient numbers of school teachers and university staff to dispense with Egyptians and to make the domain of education the almost exclusive preserve of local Arabs, many of whom have received research training abroad, and who are already emerging as a very distinctive category.

Whether one thinks of the past or the present, therefore, it is of fundamental importance to take cognisance of the diversity that has existed and still exists. Emphasis must be given to this because the crude dichotomy is so frequently drawn between the towns and "the outside" *(al-barr)*, citizens and bedouin, state and tribal organisations. This has come about partly as a result of administrative usage, past and present, but also by the usage common among people themselves. If it is to mean nothing more than a settled as against a tented way of life, the dichotomy is permissable. Agostini, for example, produced excellent surveys in two volumes, of the populations of Cyrenaica, Tripolitania and Fezzan, although the details for the latter pair are recorded on the basis of territorial divisions, and the former on the basis of tribal divisions, the structure of the analysis is the same in all three cases; it is based on local kin groups forming divisions of tribes. Comparing the two volumes, interesting conceptual differences appear in them. Thus in Tripolitania the words *Luhma* and *Batn* are used in reference to divisions of a tribe, while in Cyrenaica the words *Bayt* and

'Ait are used for these divisions. That is to say, in Tripolitania both concepts are essentially feminine, meaning flesh and womb respectively, while both Cyrenaican terms refer to people, presumed to be kin, gathered together under the religious shelter of a *Bayt*, a special sort of tent top which has the *Baraka* (divine goodness) of wool in it, and which, within the precincts delimited by its ropes, is *Haram* (sacred). By extension, the work is used to include the people of a camp, and, further the cluster of camps occupying the same small tribal territory. More pointedly, perhaps, is the common use, among Cyrenaican bedouin, of the term *'Amara Dam'* to designate "those people who have agreed to live together and to pay blood money together", to quote the exegetical gloss that a bedouin offered me and to mean, in anthropological language, the members of a local corporate group; in Tripolitania the phrase is virtually unknown. These are not linguistic problems only, for kinship usages and accompanying forms of behaviour differ in relation to these conceptual modes of thinking about groupings of people. Thus, in Tripolitania, the descendants of maternal half brothers are categorised as patrilineal kin, while among Cyrenaican bedouin this is never done. Moreover, these conceptual differences and differences of kindship categorisation are both reflected in rights of heirship: in Tripolitania a man has right of access to the resources of his mother's natal group; in Cyrenaica a man might use the resources of his mother's natal group, but by its grace *(b'il-fadal)* only, and not of right. In matters of the constitution of local groups, the control of resources, and the transmission of rights to those of succeeding generations, in all these important matters of social organisation, the three provinces have always gone their separate ways.

Against this stress put here on the dissimilarities in social organisation it might be argued that the central unit throughout the land has been the tribe. Justification for this comes from the accurate claim that the word *Qabila* is used as a designation for the larger groups of people in all three provinces, and that for this reason an aspect of social organisation is common to them all. Further, since major units are comparable, their constituent parts must bear some similarity. Neither of these two conclusions follow, any more than it would be tenable to argue that the universal use of the word house in England indicated a like unit for the aristocracy and the rest of the population. The ubiquity which inheres in the word *Qabila* means that it occurs widely in the Middle East, in a vast range of differing circumstances, applied to groups in towns, villages, and camps, to men with numerous sons alike to tens of thousands of people, regardless of any of the details of social organisation. In parts of the Middle East, as in Libya, it can also refer to the people inhabiting a more backward area of a country, or to a remote area largely unknown to townspeople, or as a mark of distinction for the indigenous population in a small country where it is in control of the government but numerically threatened to be overwhelmed by immigrants. Given this latitude and elasticity of meaning, enabling it to contract or expand contextually, then it is plain folly to assume similarity of organisation wherever the word is applied.

Tacitly, those who have adopted this assumption accept that in climatically marginal arid areas, where the technology is rudimentary, the relation of people to their environment is so close as to constitute a natural fit, of such sophisticated adjustment that the response is the only possible option: in short, a tribal system. There are anthropologists who postulate certain pre-requisites for the development of certain types of social organisation, so that if all (or even some) of these prerequisites are known, the social institutions can be deduced. In a sense so broad as to be almost meaningless, Libya can be characterised by its aridity, by an unstable rainfall regime in the amounts that fall annually and in the variations from place to place in each year, by a lack of continuous vegetation, by a shortage of water, and by a dearth of building materials in many of its parts. Taken together, these prerequisites necessitate a low density of population, dispersed in small groups, engaged in pastoralism, and catching a cereal crop wherever and whenever possible: the essential elements of tribal system in fact. This being so, it can be assumed that unless there has been a change in natural resources, leading to an increase or decline in the population, this tribal system has persisted unchanged over a very long period. Although not a determinist, but one who has argued against the idea of necessary prerequisites for types of social organisation, Evans-Pritchard (1949), in his history of *The Sanusi of Cyrenaica*, after a somewhat vague reference to possible changes prior to the beginning of the nineteenth century, depicts the social organisation of Cyrenaica as a segmentary tribal system in a condition of stasis from then onwards, or at least until he arrived in the country and near the time of the return of Sayyid Idris (as he then was), later to become Emir, and the formation of a State began. It is not the intention to offer a criticism of Evans-Pritchard's history but, simply to point out that since he was still thinking in terms of an overarching social system, without supposing that the Cyrenaican tribal system was uniformly spread throughout the country and that it had persisted unchanged for at least the century of the Sanusi Order's history, his analysis would lose its validity. This remark, indeed, holds true for any structural type of analysis of a social system, since the analysis itself can only be pursued by assuming stasis, whether this assumption is held as a heuristic fiction, or as a belief that structural changes are impossible without the intrusion of an external factor.

There have, of course, always been intrusions of this sort. In 1788 'An Association for promoting Discovery in the Inland parts of Africa' was founded in London, and in 1798 Hornemann, sponsored by the Association, left Cairo and travelled through Siwa and Jalu to Marzuq, and thence to Tripoli. In the early nineteenth century, Tripoli became the platform from which expeditions were mounted, sponsored by the British Government, to prospect for trans-Saharan trade routes. At the time, the famous and powerful Yusaf Karamanli was able to exert sufficient control over the Fezzan to secure the safe passage of caravans and travellers across the Sahara to Bornu, Niger, and other parts of West Africa. As a result of all these activities across and deep into the Fezzan, Manchester cotton goods soon found their way into West Africa, both via Morocco and Tripoli. According to the accounts, the volume of trade was substantial, the caravans huge, the number of slaves travelling these routes ran into thousands of people to each caravan, and the quantities of goods shifted northwards from West Africa, matched by manufactured goods taken southwards, were sufficiently important to the then foremost industrial country in the world, for it to expend large sums on exploratory expeditions and to maintain a trade consulate deep in the Sahara.

It is necessary to relate this, not for its intrinsic historical interest but because some sort

of secure provision was required to ensure the safe
passage of goods and slaves over such vast distances.
It is inconceivable that traders would have risked
caravans with their thousands of human beings and
valuable goods - gold among them - unless there was
a measure of control over the desert routes, and that
on arrival in Marzuq arrangements for their accom-
modation had been made in advance. Clearly, there
had to be organisation throughout the length of
these trade routes if the effort were to be worth
while. There had to be men of considerable power
throughout Fezzan and Tripolitania to provide the
necessary facilities at the caravan staging posts;
but their function was not merely to provide and
maintain these caravanserai, they also had to afford
protection at these places, and for the caravans on
their outward journeys - and this in turn meant the
command of large bodies of men. The barons of Brach,
Sabhah, Marzuq, and the redoubtable Saif an-Nasr
group of the Aulad Sulaiman, familiar to us as living
figures, had their roots in this earlier period of
the more shadowy big men, who were the organisers of
groups for the control of long distant trade, and
not in a tribal segmentary system. Hence, Agostini,
writing more than half a century later, perforce
presents his population survey on a territorial
basis, the names of which were familiar to the
early explorers and controllers of caravans as
delineating their routes; he also refers to the
administrative division, the *caza*, and gives some of
the names of leaders in them. He records too the
larger political units of *Saff al-Bahar* (the coastal
alignment), and *Saff al-Fauqi* (the interior alignment), *Sufuf* (alignments) composed of loose groupings
of people to form leagues, largely for the defence
of mutual interests when there was a general threat
to a wider territory. This stands in marked con-
trast to his population survey of Cyrenaica, which
is done on a tribal basis, where members of sections
were highly concentrated on their own territories.
In Tripolitania and Fezzan the named stock groups
(a designation which is preferable to tribes) were
scattered higgledy-piggledy over the countryside,
and not genealogically articulated, as were the
Cyrenaicans, under the status conferring umbrella
of Sa'ada, the founding ancestress of them all.

Towards the middle of the nineteenth century,
a profound change came over the trans-Saharan trade
in the area in which, until then, it had plied. Two
main developments affected it. First, throughout
the eighteen forties, the English Government put

pressure on the Turks to suppress the slave trade and, although it was not finally ended until the late nineteen twenties - Rosita Forbes mentions young children being smuggled in caravans as slaves in 1920/21 - despite the efforts of the Sanusi, the volume of slave traffic decreased rapidly by 1857. Secondly, almost coincidental with the decrease in slave trading, the increasing use of the steam ship meant that trade between Europe and West Africa became, more and more, by sea routes. In 1859, the German Heine, visiting Tripoli, remarked on the decline of the port and the falling off of imports. Bovill, in his *Caravans of the Old Sahara*, ends his account of trans-Sahara trade at about this time; and his map showing the principal caravan routes of the nineteenth century gives only those in the western half of the Sahara, from the line Tripoli-Mizdah-Marzuq-Bilma westwards to the Atlantic. In that area, trade suffered a spectacular drop, but far from declining throughout the Sahara, it was switched to the eastern Sahara; for the trans-Sahara routes were still by far the quickest way of transporting goods to Egypt and beyond. Some of the Fezzanes caravanseri still continued to flourish, but the centrally positioned oasis of Kufrah now became the hub of trade, routes leaving it in many directions, like the spokes of a wheel.

When these changes in commerce were taking place, there appeared in Cyrenaica the founder of the Sanusi Order, in 1842. His Order had already got underway, for he had established lodges in Arabia and Egypt before Cyrenaica and, incidently, had won the strong support of the future Sultan of Wadai, Muhammad Sharif, while they were together at Mecca. The first lodge in Cyrenaica was built at al-Bayda and soon they appeared in some profusion on the Jabal al-Akhdar. The Grand Sanusi, as the founder was called, died in 1859, but before his demise he had registered some remarkable achievements. Two are of particular concern in this context. First, he moved his seat to the inhospitable, mosquito infested, and poor oasis of Jaghbub, and, with voluntary labour - some of it consisting of freed slaves, it is said - he converted it into the home of a thriving community, and a centre of learning. The oasis at that time was in Egypt, it was astride the pilgrimage route to Mecca and on the route from Siwa southwards. More importantly perhaps, the example he set in cleaning the place, providing for travellers and creating for these a sense of security and order, was one that

was to be urged upon other oasis dwellers. In the
letters he and his successor, Sayyid Mahdy, sent to
those who supplicated for a lodge, the need to keep
it clean and to maintain it in proper order was
stressed, and to these supplicants, as to other
followers, the strong advice was given to worship
God, to give shelter to wayfarers, and to abjure
brigandage. The oases of the eastern Sahara, the
stepping stones along the trade routes which had
been given a new impetus about this time, were
henceforward to promote the flow of trade, not to
impede it, on the direct instructions of the Head
of the Sanusi Order.

Second, and closely linked to the first, it is
noteworthy that the Grand Sanusi captured the
allegiance of the trans-Saharan traders, the Zuwaya
groups of people. Quite what their position was at
this time I do not know, but it is most likely that
their activities, increased by the switch in trade,
were greatly stimulated by their Sanusi connection.
Writers have speculated on the reason for the Grand
Sanusi moving his seat out of the bedouin area of
Cyrenaica to an oasis some 200 miles south of
Tubruq. A desire to get away from Turkish influence
is the explanation offered by some. A desire to
live a quite life devoted to contemplation is offered
by others. In Evans-Pritchard's view the Grand
Sanusi aimed for externality vis-à-vis the tribes
of Cyrenaica and, from this newly found neutrality,
the Order was better positioned to penetrate them.
It would be too much of a diversion here to offer a
critique of these explanations, particularly the
latter, by far the most thought-provoking of them.
Suffice it to say that Jaghbub was a route junction,
that the Grand Sanusi captured the allegiance of,
by now, a famous group of traders, that in 1845 he
had begun his penetration of south Tripolitania,
with a lodge at Mizdah, and that soon after he had
found his way into the Fezzan; add to this his
successor's moves, first to Kufrah and then to Quru
in Chad, and it immediately appears astonishing that
authors have had the temerity to concoct explanations
of the Sanusi's moves when this brief account of his
activities makes the answer cartographically plain
for all to see. The aim was to gain the allegiance
of the traders in the Saharan oases, and to spread
the Order along their trade routes, southwards into
the much more densely populated Sudan and West
Africa.

Thus far, reference has been made to some of
the more conspicuous differences in social organisa-

tion between the three provinces, and to the changes which affected them during the nineteenth century. I now wish to look a little closer at some of the differences within Cyrenaica itself, and begin with the trading group referred to previously, the Zuwaya peoples. They did not constitute a tribe in the sense that the word *Qabila* was applied to other units referred to in this way. In a technical sense, the Zuwaya were clients of the Magharba tribe, and each of its sections claimed a group of the Zuwaya as its particular clients. Thus, the Julilat group of Zuwaya was attached to the Nasr section of the Magharba. The connection was still recognised until recently, and its effectiveness is seen in the fact that members of the Julilat living in Kufrah tended and dealt with the date palms growing there, which were owned by people of the Nasr section. But the Zuwaya people were also powerful in that they were the keepers of the keys to the Sahara and controlled its trade routes. Ajadabiyah was the northern terminus of their trade connections, and, near what used to be a small township with its *funduq* (animal market), over 200 tents were dispersed in some three camps, when I lived among them in 1948. Southwards they had connections through the oases of Jalu and Awjilah to Kufrah (where they were gathered in strength) and thence to Wadai, Chad, Zinder and Kano. The effectiveness of these links can be seen from the fact that one of their shaikhs, in 1948, personally collected contributions to a blood money payment he was required to make, from relatives in five of the places mentioned, including Chad and Wadai. What is more, this blood money was made over in one payment, to end the affair, a practice rarely adopted by Cyrenaican tribes. Yet there was no great leader with a wide span of power. In Ajadabiyah there was a shaikh who styled himself Omda, and was encouraged in this by his immediate followers. Literate in Italian as a result of his dealings with Italian officialdom during its occupation of the country, his pretentions were denied by other Zuwaya, although the expertise he had gained from his dealings with governmental offices impressed many. The nature of his power was, however, quite unlike that of some of the big men of the Fezzan in its scale, and unlike that of bedouin shaikhs who, if they were to progress in power, first had to capture the allegiance of the corporate group to which they belonged. Moreover, the Zuwaya were not territorially concentrated, but dispersed widespread throughout the eastern Saharan oases, and beyond into West Africa. If the word tribe is to be applied to them, it must be in an ethnic not in a structural sense. Thus, in Cyrenaica, there lived a group of people, specialists in long distant trade, whose widely flung connections were related to the needs arising out of this specialism, whose social organisation was uniquely different to that of any other group.

Two other examples, of the differences which obtained between groups of people in Cyrenaica, are now cited briefly. A group of the Nasr section of the Maghaba tribe owned a small strip of territory only a few miles in length and under two miles wide. The territory was almost completely lacking in any kind of ecological diversity. The total population of the group was as little as 200 in round figures. Obviously, were this group to achieve a minimum of economic stability it had urgent need for regular access to the resources of other corporate groups. For such is the nature of the ecology that, in any particular year, a particular small area of territory might be enjoying optimum rainfall conditions - and hence a full well and abundant crop returns - while an adjacent area of territory might be experiencing virtual drought conditions, with well water in short supply, and the crop stunted or a total failure. It is urgently necessary, therefore, for groups to be able to tap the surplus resources of others when they themselves are suffering a deficit in any given year. Put in another way, each group needs durable connections with other groups, so that when the need arises claims can be made on their resources - the need is so imperative that it cannot be left to the frailty of good will or favours. Marriage is the means for ensuring the recognition of claims to resources, and the details of the marriage patterns of groups serve as a reliable measure of their economic and political strength. The marriages of the men and women of this group were patterned in such fashion as to provide the group with water for animal needs from several other corporate groups, and more distant connections enabled them to grow a cereal crop of sorts each year whatever vicissitudes afflicted them in any particular year. Reciprocal marriages had also been forged between them and people in the date oases of Zillah and Maradah, and each year men went to collect dates, returning in September when the dates were crucial in eking out their meagre diet at a time of the year when milk and meat were not yet available; they also sold some of their dates in Ajadabiyah to buy sugar, tea, some other foods and clothes. The group was economically well placed, producing a surplus to its needs, of which it could dispose. But, although its population was small, it was demographically favourable in that the number of able-bodied young men and women was disproportionately large and, for this reason, its senior men aspired to power positions which they had not previously enjoyed. Limits were, nevertheless, set to this expansion of power because the group was dependent on its external connections, although these had been skilfully planned and concentrated in six other corporate groups. Two options were open to the group in its quest for power. Either it could engage in aggressive action and take territory from neighbours by force, an unlikely option in the late forties and early fifties; or it could make its linked groups so dependent as to achieve dominance for itself. Thus, by patterning its social relationships in the manner briefly described, this group etched out a micro-structure of power which positioned it to hold sway over several similar groups. This is a pattern which characterises groups of similar power span among camel-herders.

At the lower end of the power scale, a weak group has its external connections dissipated in a large number of groups, these marriages uniting spouses of similar poverty. It is also a feature of such groups that a significant portion of their marriage assets are expended on marriages to poor client groups.

At the other end of the scale, to come now to the second example, the development of very large-scale power has occurred. One of the most famous of Cyrenaican groups provides an apposite example. I refer to the Hadduth group of the Bara'asa. Its chief, as it is appropriate to call him, was the renowned Bu Bakr, a *Mudir* under the Turks in the mid-nineteenth century, who lived in a castle near Fa'idiyah and who, when Hamilton paid him a visit, was surrounded by retainers, and who is reported to have dominated a large area in central Cyrenaica. The key to the scale of power held by this group lies in the extent of territory it occupied. Bedouin of central Cyrenaica recognise three main ecological zones in that part of the country. First, there is the Green Mountain *(al-Jabal al-Akhdar)*, so called because the vegetation there is

Cultural and Social Diversity in Libya

continuous. The climate is of a Mediterranean type. The animals kept are mainly cows and goats. Cultivation of cereals is regular, on plots cleared and fertilised in late summer by slash and burn techniques. Second, lying south of the *Jabal* is the area known as the *Sirwal* (Turkish trousers). Topographically, it is characterised by low lying, rather narrow tongues of land protruding southwards from the mountains: the mountain area is likened to the baggy seat of a Turkish trousers, and the tongues of land to its narrow legs. Here the aridity is much greater, the vegetation consisting uniformly of low succulent bushes, and cultivation is of a catch-crop kind. Camels and sheep make their appearance in this zone. Third, there is the *Sha'afa*, an area of wide open level stretches, ideal for camels. Vegetation for the dry eight months of the year is confined to succulants (like the huge thistles) that grow in depressions, but, when the rainfall is favourable, the crop returns that can be produced on the fertile loess soils are truly amazing. The inhabitants of this area, like their animals, are highly mobile. South of the *Sha'afa* lies the *Sarir*, the barren and uninhabited desert proper. The group's territory stretches from Bayda/Massa south into the *Sha'afa*, to the every edge of the desert. Within this unusual longitudinal length of territory is included a range of ecological diversity not possessed by any other corporate group. Such assets as these allowed a population expansion of over 700, not counting clients, when I lived among the Hadduth people in 1949/50. Economically secure, and with a population sufficiently large to provide spouses for most of its members, it was able to be much more discriminate in its connections, of course, but since these were not urgently required for purposes of economic stability, they could be used for political advantage. It is not surprising that as the country moved to independence, it had among its members the Minister of the Interior, later to become Foreign Minister and Prime Minister of Libya; the Chief of Police, later to become Field Marshal of the Libyan police force; a member of Parliament; and the *Mushtashar* of the Bara'asa tribe, not to mention lesser positions, or the high positions held by affinal relatives. Also, some of the distinguished names mentioned by Evans-Pritchard as great warriors in the wars against the Italians came from this group.

Here, only three sorts of patterns of social

organisations have been discussed. Were I to refer to plateau tribes proper, such as the Darsa, among three sections of which I lived in 1950, more profound differences in the patterning of social relationships would become evident. I hope that those patterns I have discussed will suffice to allow me to make the point that to subsume these fundamental differences under a single segmentary tribal organisation is not only misleading but relates little to any groups anywhere. For, at the core of the theory of segmentary systems is the idea that segments, at any order of division, are homologus. The point here is that the adoption of this idea leads to gross inaccuracy. An approach to an understanding of bedouin life is through the characteristic patternsof relationships, not through an all embracing segmentary system.

Thus far the argument has been directed to validating the view that at any particular period in Libya's history, multiple patterns of arrangements existed, depending largely on individual perception of various interests, and the attempts individuals made to configure their social relationships to further these. Since these perceptions change as circumstances alter, patterns of social relationships are re-configured historically. In both a contemporary and historical sense, therefore, multiple patterns of social relationships appear, so that the pattern for a particular group or cluster of groups, at one time, might be a league of small corporate groups, and, at another time, a *de facto* chiefship, and, at yet another time, a small impoverished group dependent on others and shorn of its power.

I wish not to turn to the post oil period. I cannot speak of this with the same confidence as the period immediately leading to independence, because I have done only one year's fieldwork in Libya in this period, and three recent visits were too short to conduct systematic enquiries. I can, consequently do little other than list the issues which seem important to me.

The most obvious issue is the migration of people away from the pastoral areas to swell the population of settled people. It has occurred in two waves. The first began in the late forties, when small numbers of bedouin, sensing that an administration, staffed by Libyans for the first time in centuries, held prospects of a relationship with settled areas of a kind previously unknown, moved into what were then small villages: places

Cultural and Social Diversity in Libya

like al-Abiyar and Ajadabiyah. Many bedouin boys, unschooled at the time, now occupy a number of diverse positions, simply because men of their parental generation had the foresight to move. The second migration, much larger and more widespread than the first, almost emptied the semi-desert areas in places. In some areas - the *Sirwal* and *Sha'afa* areas in Cyrenaica for example - people abandoned catch cropping, the main body of a corporate group decamping to settle around Massa, leaving only a few experienced shepherds and herdsmen to care for the animals. The amount of the population able to leave after the abandonment of catch cropping is a good index of the proportion of the bedouin labour force, tied unproductively for some ten months of the year to the semi-desert, required to sustain the cereal growing component of the economy in the past: where there had been about a dozen camps of 5 to 10 tents in 1950, in one central area, the number of camps, by 1969, had been reduced to two, or three tents each.

Although it is readily appreciated that a move into the vicinity of, say, al-Abiyar is not the same as a move into a farm on the olive plantation of al-Khadara - the economy is different in both cases, the division of labour is different, the relation between the sexes is different, and the pattern of marriage (and hence the significance of affinity) is different - migration in Libya has a sufficient general similarity about it to mark it as notably unlike the same phenomenon in other parts of Africa. In Central Africa, migration drove people across cultural and linguistic boundaries to industries, and the problems and institutions which emerged are anchored in this two prime facts. In Libya, there was an absence of a cultural barrier, the bedouin did not enter industry, and the process of settling was not beset with difficulties: they had long been accustomed to shuffling around in search for resources, and where they found them they remained in an area for as long as they held out. Settled life is an indefinite prolongation of part of a way of life with which they were well familiar from the past.

Third, the aim of massive spending on technological developments is to alter resources, especially water. The first revolution, in this largely semi-desert country, was in classical times, when elaborate underground cisterns were constructed to store water. The aim now is to stimulate a second revolution by building numerous dams to increase vastly the amount of distributable water on a permanent basis, and thus to begin the march against the desert, by extending the periphery of those areas under established cultivation. It might be a loosing battle: studies show that the rising level of sea water in the water table is already a serious threat (see chapter 3). Such is the pressure on water resources as a result of the growth in the settled population, that the dams may serve only to assist in maintaining the sweet water level. Over reliance on superior technological arrangements can, moreover, be disasterous. After a succession of drought years in the late forties in Tripolitania, the irrigation system was brought to a standstill, with the threat of near famine conditions, and the migration of thousands of people into Cyrenaica; while the bedouin, there, not anchored to any particular acreage by irrigation, moved around, and met the challenge of climatic vagaries in a more naturally resourceful manner. For technological advances to be of enduring worth, they must be such as to dominate nature, no matter what vissititudes with which it capricuously inflicts human beings.

Fourth, as bedouin boys have grown to maturity some have become farmers, others traders, government officials of different sorts and rank, they have also entered into higher education and become professionals. Where previously occupational differentiation was irrelevant it has become characteristic. The effect has been felt in all social units, including the elementary family, and since marriages tend to follow peoples interests, the direction of change in patterns of marriage are already discernable. Ex-bedouin who, in 1948, scorned town and village connections, have married the daughters of administrators, and others have married into professional families of newly acquired status. The more successful *shaikhs*, who have diversified their links to the maximum permitted by the past pastoral economy, are precisely those who have enlarged the diversity of their connections, now permitted by the contemporary increase in social differentiation.

Fifth, the availability of bank loans, first at preferential rates and, by 1965, free of interest, for buying olive farms, machinery and so on, had the quite unintended effect of virtually collapsing the leadership which had existed. The *shaikh* of the corporate group was no longer the person to mediate the individual relationships of his followers, for they now had direct access to different kinds of resources than those over which he had exercised control earlier. Men of much greater power than these shaiks also suffered dimunition of status as the shaiks, their bedouin props, lost theirs. One of the most powerful men in Cyrenaica in 1950, as early as 1964 expressed confusion about the distribution of power in all three territories, which he admitted he could no longer comprehend. The anomie, to use Durkheimian idiom, in the field of power at least, was, in the mid-sixties, quite striking.

Sixth, as oil royalties began to mount from 1962 onwards, the *sharika* or patrnership made its appearance. *Ad hoc* initially, these groups had permanance about them, since they consisted of people who had agreed to contribute together half the cost of a venture, and share the other half of the costs as a bank loan. The composition of these partnerships provides the opportunity for a fascinating piece of research. Here I mention only one aspect of their constitution. Many, in their memberships, straddle settled and pastoral groups, therby maximising the economic advantages of both. For oil has not brought pastoralism to an end. The increase in cost of animals has been dramatic: a fat sheep cost about £L3 to £L4 in 1948, but by the mid-seventies it cost over LD150, and the cost of a *jamal ghalid* (a big strong camel) rose from £L15/18 to over LD500 during the same period. These increases have given a new lease of life to pastoralism, albeit a different sort of life, by making it worthwhile still to keep animals in the semi-desert, and, here and there, to use areas for camel herding previously considered to be too arid.

Seventh, and finally, throughout the seventies there has been a gradual but persistent shift from the collective ownership of land by local corporate groups to individual ownership. To my mind, this has been the most fundamental change, certainly among the camel cum sheep people of Cyrenaica. Appeals by individual bedouin to have their corporate share of land detached from the corporate body are increasingly granted by the courts, and this novel concept of landownership has become enshrined in a series of enactments. Until the fifties there was no such thing as an individual share of land, only rights of usufruct to corporately owned land. As a result of this one change, the corporate group has not been modified, it has not merely evolved, it has been collapsed. With its disappearance the obstacle to settling the people of the romany way of life will be removed. And with the irrevocable settlement of people, governing the country will soon become a different matter; for those of us with experience of bedouin life know full well how very difficult it has been to control groups of people when they are here today and gone tomorrow.

It would appear that all these changes have produced a uniformity of social organisation, and the universal partnerships as the characteristic mode of group organisation. Research will show, I am confident, that the composition, constitution, and function of these partnerships will reveal a variety of patterns as diverse as those of the past. It is more impelling, perhaps, than previously, that the use if a simplistic model of a single social structure is abandoned in favour of the search of characteristic patterns of behaviour, capable of comprehending larger areas of reality.

Notes

1. Allan, J.A., 1979, 'Managing agricultural resources in Libya: recent experience', *Libyan Studies*, Vol X, pp 17-28
2. Abu Boahen, A., 1964, *Britain, the Sahara and the Western Sudan*, Clarendon Press, Oxford
3. Barth, H., 1857, *Travels and Discoveries in North and Central Africa*, Longmans, Brown, Green and Roberts, London
4. Bovill, E.W., 1933, *Caravans of the old Sahara*, Oxford University Press, London
5. De Agostini, E., 1917 *Le Popolazioni Della Tripolitania*, Governo Della Tripolitania, Tripoli
6. De Agostini, E., 1922/23, *Le Popolazioni Della Cirenaica*, Governo Della Cirenaica, Benghazi
7. Denham D. and Clapperton, H., 1826, *Narrative of Travels and Discoveries in Northern and Central Africa*, Murray, London
8. Evans-Pritchard, E.E., 1949, *The Sanusi of Cyrenaica*, Clarendon Press, Oxford
9. Forbes, R., 1921, *The Secret of the Sahara: Kufrah*, Cassell, London
10. Hamilton, J., 1856, *Wanderings in North Africa*, Murray, London
11. Horneman, F., 1802, *The Journal of Frederick Horneman's Travels from Cairo to Marzuq*, Nicol, London
12. Lyons, G.F., 1821, *A Narrative of Travels in Northern Africa*, Murray, London
13. Richardson, J., 1853, *Narrative of a Mission to Central Africa*, Chapman and Hall, London

14. Wright, J., 1969, *Libya*, Benn, London

Chapter 9

THE POLITICAL DEVELOPMENT OF LIBYA 1952-1969: INSTITUTIONS, POLICIES AND IDEOLOGY

Salaheddin Hasan Sury

INTRODUCTION

The Libyan political system during the period 1952-1969 was based on the Libyan Constitution of 7 October 1951, which was worked out by an appointed National Assembly of sixty members representing evenly the three provinces of Libya - Cyrenaica, Fezzan and Tripolitania. The constitution took into consideration the necessary compromises made by the three separate entities, with their local particularism, their socio-economic differences, and their distinct interests.[1]

Cyrenaica was predominantly a tribal society, most of whose tribes were linked together and further united by their strong adherence to the 'Sanusiyya Tarika', whose last recognised *Shaikh*, Idris al Sanusi, became the undisputed leader of the province. Under the auspices of the British, Idris was recognised on 1 June 1949 as the *Amir* of the autonomous Amirate of Cyrenaica, which eventually developed its own constituency, legal system, and various government organs.[2] Fezzan, the desert province in the south, had a tiny population of different ethnic background scattered over a vast arid territory. There the Saif al Nasr family of Arab origin had fought the Turks and the Italians and later achieved a conspicious position under the French in the post Second World War period.[3] Tripolitania supported the largest segment of population, was the most urbanised and modernised. The majority of its population lived a settled life as peasants, merchants, workers, and craftsmen. It was torn by area, town, and family rivalries which found some expression in the political parties allowed by the British. Shortly before independence on 24 December 1951, a position crystallised with an

Political developments 1952-1969

Istiklal Party, which finally endorsed federalism as adopted by the National Assembly, and a Congress Party, which formed the opposition and advocated a unitary system.[4]

Thus Cyrenaica, which was heading towards statehood under the Sanusi, was in a stronger position than a divided Tripolitania, which was still directly under the British administration. Cyrenaica was able to put forward its preconditions for any unity with Tripolitania, and therefore it presented federalism, Idris as the monarch for the prospective state, and Benghazi as its capital, as practically unnegotiable provisions. Fezzan with its small scattered population was of very little effect in this respect, though it shared Cyrenaica's suspicions that unconditional unity with Tripolitania might lead eventually to their liquidation.[5]

All those major preconditionas were accepted by the Tripolitanians as the price for unity. They accepted even the idea of two capitals: Tripoli and Benghazi. Many more problems arose in the course of the debate at the Assembly, in which the Tripolitanians showed remarkable flexibility. Finally on 24 December 1951, Idris declared the independence of Libya according to the United Nations Resolution of 21 November 1949, under its new formal name, The United Kingdom of Libya.[6]

THE LIBYAN INSTITUTIONS

The Federal system as drawn up by the National Assembly continued until 7 December 1962. It was based on the fragmentation of power amongst the palace, officials, the organs of the federal government, and the organs of the provincial government. The King was the head of the state and the supreme commander-in-chief of the armed forces. He had several privileges according to the constitution such as the appointment and dismissal of senior officials. He was inviolable and exempted from any responsibility, though by virtue of his position as the King, he acquired a special status as the ultimate authority in the country.[7] He was assisted by the Royan Diwan, or palace cabinet, with a chief, two deputies, and several other officials, often engaged in power struggles with the federal government. There was also the position of *Nazir al Khassa*, or the chief of the royal household, which was always directed by the Shalhi family which had been in the service of Idris since his early childhood, and whose members were involved in the power struggles and in the Sanusi rivalries.[8]

The federal government was constituted of the cabinet or the council of ministers, the Parliament with its two houses, and the supreme court whose judges were appointed for life. The lower house, whose members were elected, was dominated by the Tripolitanians while the Senate represented evenly the three provinces, half its members were appointed by the King, while the rest were elected through the legislative councils of the provinces. The cabinet members were collectively and individually responsible before the House of Representatives.[9] The federal government was in charge of foreign affairs, defence, customs, postal system, and shared power with the provinces in various economic, financial, educational and legal matters.[10]

The provincial political system was made up of a Wali representing the King, and an executive council appointed by the King, and a legislative council most of whom were elected.[11] Policies were implemented and services were rendered through an expanding civil service administration. Bureaucracy which had been started under the Ottomans in the 1860s had steadily grown under the succeeding regimes. The federal government and the three provinces had their own bureaucracies.

Each state had its own police force, and the federal government had its own symbolic force which dealt with matters related to federal and inter-state affairs. In addition to their normal police activities, the Tripolitanian Police Force and the Cyrenaican Defence Force symbolised the power of the state prior to the establishment of the Libyan army and served as semi-provincial armies in their respective areas. They were considered as the source of the regime's security and continuity in power since they checked underground activities, suppressed violent demonstrations, helped the regime to control elections, and provided a safeguard against any possible takeover by the army.[12]

The Libyan army was created in 1953, and was staffed by some veterans of the Sanusi army and by some young officers who were hastily trained in a special centre established in Zawiyah a year later. It was eventually dominated by young officers who studied in military academies both in Libya and abroad. The regime viewed the army with suspicion; therefore it tried to keep it out of politics, placing its command in the hands of loyal old Sanusi veterans.[13]

Political developments 1952-1969

It was for political reasons that Idris revived several traditional religious institutions and introduced them in modern form. He established in 1952 a higher religious college in al Baydah where the Grand Sanusi started his first *Zawiya* in 1843. It was developed later into an Islamic University with a special religio-political status which involved it in power politics. Idris also reactivated the Sanusi *zawiyas* which were administered like government offices with salaried staff, completely different from the original autonomous and self-administered form.[14]

The struggle between the King, the federal government and the provinces started during the early days of independence, and involved several legal interpretations, both in the constitutions and in the organic laws of the provinces.[15] There was also continuing attacks from the advocates of the unitary system, who introduced federalism as an imposed dividing phenomenon against the natural unity of the *Umma*. Others deplored the fact that the meagre resources of the country, which came mainly from foreign aid and which should have been spent on development, were being wasted in supporting four governments.[16]

Towards the end of the first decade the general public attitude was in favour of the abrogation of the federal system. There was a general feeling that it was time to take action in that direction, since the country had so far received more social integration as a result of mixtures of population through the federal government, the university, the armed forces, and in various social and economic activities. There was also pressure from the new generation, whose aspirations went even beyond the limits of the Libyan boundaries. On 7 December 1962 the constitution was amended and the political status of the province was abolished. The provinces were turned into large administrative units with a *Wali* and an administrative council for each unit.[17]

The process of unification was, however, accomplished on 25 April 1963, when the position of the *Wali* and the administrative council were abolished and the Kingdom was reorganised into its final unified form. It was divided into ten administrative units called *muhafadah*, governances. Each *muhafadah* was governed by an appointed *muhafaz*, chosen from the professional politicians, but later recruited from the rank and file of the bureacracy. Each *muhafadah* had its own consultative council and was divided into *baladiyat*, municipalities, each of which had its own appointed mayor and municipal council.[18] Necessary changes were made to adapt all the federal, political and administrative institutions to the new unitary form of the state.(see map, Figure 7, p136)

THE POLICIES OF THE STATE

King Idris established the basis of the state policies during the period 1952-1969. He consolidated his position in the country, preserved an equilibrium among the provinces, and kept intact the balance between the various political factions. Internationally, he cautiously followed an undeclared pro-Western policy, took a moderate Arab stand, and kept normal relations with the rest of the world. In all he followed a policy of the least direct involvement.

King Idris realised that he had been accepted as the King of All Libya through compromise, since in the province of Tripolitania the *Sanusiyya* was either unknown or unpopular. On the other hand he owed his position as the undisputed leader in Cyrenaica and the *de facto* leader of the whole of Libya to the *Sanusi* movement. Thus, at the very time when he had to act as a secular leader with no guide other than the constitution, he had to keep his position as *Sanusi* leader and *Shaikh* of a *Tarika*. It was,therefore, not mere coincidence that he revived and reactivated the religious *Sanusi* institutions referred to earlier.[19]

Idris, furthermore, consolidated his power by the total arrest, banishment, and imprisonment of the members of the Sanusi household as an immediate reaction to the assassination of his life companion, Ibrahim al Shalhi, the *Nazir* of the royal household on 5 October 1954, by a member of the Sanusi family.[20] While consolidating his power and having gradually and steadily gathered all the affairs of the state in his own grip, he was careful to do this from behind the scenes, avoiding any open involvement in everyday politics. He tried to impress his image among the people in a paternal way and became a myth in their memories.[21]

He started his work by banning political parties and outlawing any originated opposition. In February 1952, following the first parliamentary election, the National Congress Party of Tripolitania, which advocated the form of a unitary state, was dissolved, its property was confiscated, and its leaders were either deported or imprisoned.[22] The free press was also banned, and only government newspapers were permitted. Later some newspapers were allowed on an individual basis, but without the right to criticise the government's fundamental policies.[23] In the absence of political parties and recognised and organised opposition, policies were implemented through the interplay of personalities, frequent changes of faces, and immediate action and reaction.

The cabinet, though formed by the prime minister, always included members named by the palace for the balance of power, and they were usually sources of friction within the cabinet. Portfolios were frequently rotated among various leading personalities through continuous reshuffles and changes. It happened that within the period 1952-1969 eleven cabinets were formed, with a total of 32 reshuffles, which involved 101 ministers.[24]

As for the parliament, the 1952 elections were controlled to ensure the defeat of an opposition which endangered the federal system. In 1956, the elections were controlled to remove from the political scene members who took an opposing stand.[25] The 1960 elections were conducted with considerable freedom. New elements wer elected from businessmen, contracting, and land owning interest which had established their positions as a result of the economic prosperity which accompanied the oil companies activities. The pressure they exerted upon the government was reflected in their ability to hold an extraordinary session and discuss the possibility of a vote of no confidence in the Ku'ubar government over the famous Fezzan road crisis. Ku'ubar was dismissed and a new cabinet was formed by Bin Uthman, which absorbed part of the opposition by giving them ministerial portfolios.[26] The 1964 elections were controlled to ensure victory of the pro-government candidates by arrests of members of the opposition. When the opposition was able to organise itself among the elected members, the King dissolved parliament. The 1965 elections were controlled by breaking into the ballot boxes to ensure adoption of the pro-government candidates.[27] In general, during the first decade King Idris followed an ultra-conservative policy which intended to preserve the *status quo* of the system through the balance of power among the provinces, the federal political institutions and the various important social groups within the Libyan society, allowing for gradual changes which inevitably would come through education and economic development. However, the process of change was much faster than expected as a result of the spread of education on a very large scale and the wealth which the country gained so suddenly as a result of oil production. The political situation was accordingly altered as the new elements represented by university graduates, and in the new emerging businessmen, contractors, and land owners had their own political ambitions. Thus the second decade witnessed the confrontation between the old political elite, which was gradually declining, and the new, which was sharply rising.

King Idris proved to be very flexible in dealing with this new situation. He tried to gain supporters among the new men, and also tried to appeal to the masses through benevolent government appointments. The appointment of Dr Mohyil din Fkeni as premier on 19 March 1963 was a case in point.[28] A young educated man with a long career in politics and diplomacy, Dr Fkeni was deliberately chosen for this mission. He embarked on a very large and ambitious reform programme, but was soon caught between the high expectations and the humble realities, between the Nasser chauvinism of the Arab summit conference and the indifferent nature of the regime, and between his growing popularity and the jealousy of his fellow politicians. All these contradictory factors led to his eventual downfall amidst the student crisis of 1964, a bloody event which occurred as a result of student demonstrations in support of Fkeni and the first Arab summit conference, which provoked the police to shoot and kill several students despite the peaceful nature of the demonstrations.[29]

The King reacted by the appointment of an ultra-conservative government on 22 January 1964, with Mahmud al Muntasir as premier. However, the new elements were restored gradually through reshuffles under al Muntasir and his successor Husain Mazigh.[30] However, the major drastic action was taken when Abdul Hamid al Bakkush, a young lawyer, was named premier on 24 October 1967. Bakkush formed a cabinet of predominantly highly educated young men, and introduced well planned programmes of political, administrative, legal, and economic reform which intended to effect radical change in the Libyan political system.[31] As a result he soon fell from power, to be succeeded on 4 September 1968 by a moderate bureaucrat, Wanis al Qadhafi, who remained less than a year before the Libyan Revolution took place on 1 September 1969.

Foreign policy is not the concern of the paper, but references will be made here in brief, just to provide additional clarifying information to the state policies in its original concept. King Idris

Political developments 1952-1969

followed a very cautious foreign policy, marked by the least involvement in any international, regional, or Arab politics. Despite his strong attachment to the West, he avoided any declaration of any pro-Western stand, and never carried out any propaganda on their behalf. In the Middle East, he kept away from the exchanged attacks between Turkey and Iraq on one side and Egypt on the other over the controversial Baghdad Pact, despite his friendship with Turkey, particularly in the 1950s, and his close relations with Iraq before its 1958 revolution. He tried, as well, to keep out of any inter-Arab conflict. He remained cool and reacted quietly when the Libyan military bases were publicly criticised by President Nasser in February 1964. Through his premier Muntasir, and the unamimous vote of the parliament, the intention of ending the duration of the bases was publically declared. However, the whole issue was eventually shelved.[32]

The issue of the bases was one of the most controversial of Libyan policy during the period 1952-1969, and placed the regime under continuous attack, challenged its legitimacy, and led to its eventual downfall. Kind Idris insisted on keeping the bases and stood strong against any attempt to revise the treaties governing them. He continued to the last to view the West, particularly the British, as a source of security for his person and for his domain.[33]

The Libyan support of the Algerian Revolution (1954-1962) and its support for the Palestine cause could be pointed out as exceptional cases in Libyan politics. They should be viewed in their religio-national context with their deep roots in the consciousness of the Libyan people.

THE DEVELOPMENT OF A POLITICAL IDEOLOGY

"To preserve independence is more difficult than to get it". This simple statement by King Idris, which was later introduced as part of his "prophetic wisdom", was also an expression of the general consensus of the old political elite and their perception of the challenge which they had to face. The independence of the country, its unity, and its King, which was viewed as a national symbol, could be considered as the main elements constituting the Libyan conception of statehood in the early 1950s.[34]

This conception emerged in the absence of counter ideologies which were at that time too weak or too preoccupied to pay any attention beyond the borders of their country of origin. Furthermore, at a time when only a few countries in the Third World had achieved self-rule and most were still under colonial domination, more political independence was considered in itself a major achievement.[35]

Thus Libyanism was the focus of interest in the early 1950s. Accordingly, the process of Libyanisation was carried out successfully through schools, mass media, and various other means at the expense of provincialism, which had sharply subsided. The hopes and aspirations at that time were also of a genuine Libyan character: to turn the federal system into a unitary one and to liberate the country from foreign influence.

The situation was reversed in the late 1950s and in the 1960s, when rapid changes were taking place at various levels: international, regional and national. The bipolarity as embodied in the United States on one side and the Soviet Union on the other gradually loosened, the process of decolonisation continued on a wide scale, with several African and Asian countries declaring their independence, the rise of Nasser and the emergence of Nasserism, and the growth of the doctrinaire parties in the Arab world - all these had their effects on the traditional political ideology of the country. However, the major pressure came from within, as a result of the spread of education, which brought in new young elements into Libyan society on the one hand, and as a result of the economic changes consequent on oil production, which brought new socio-economic situations, shaking the power base of the traditional political elite on the other.

The new young elements, for example, university graduates, were influenced by political agitation in the 1950s and the 1960s. For the most part they represented political movements active in the area at that time: the Muslim Brotherhood, the Ba'ath Socialist Party, the Communist Party, and later the Arab nationalist movement. A group among them took a more realistic stance. It advocated the idea of full concentration on Libya, and the devotion of all its efforts to its welfare and development.[36] The Muslim Brotherhood was steadily declining because, with their rigid ritual requirements, political impracticability, and their clashes with Nasser in the mid-1950s, their position in Libya was accordingly weakened.[37] The other extremists, the communists, had similar problems, as they were hampered by the anti-religious and anti-national nature of their movement as well as the deterioration of its support in the area, after the Iraqi communist experiment in 1959, and the excess of their reprisals during the Kassim regime.[38]

Between these two extremes – the Muslim Brethern and the Communists – were the Ba'athists and the Arab Nationalists. They presented the Arab National idea in a philosophical framework, and therefore, they gained a relatively wider support among the intelligentsia. The growth of the Ba'athists prompted the government to take decisive action in December 1961, when it arrested 159 persons and brought them to trial. Their effort to regain power was seriously hampered by the division within the party leadership. Later, in 1963, an effort was made to revive the party's activities, and a newspaper – Al Ayyam – was issued in Tripoli. But this was soon discovered and the newspaper was suspended on 7 August 1964.[39]

The Arab Nationalist movement flourished in Libya in the early 1960s, and gained momentum after the breakdown of the Ba'ath Party. This movement was distinguished by the military training which it provided for some of its members and by its penetration of the labour force in the oil sector. This movement was also damaged by a division of opinion in its central leadership which was reflected in Libya. The activities of this secret movement were ended when in the aftermath of the June War the government arrested most of its members.[40]

The other two remaining options, which were Arab Unity and Libyan Identity, did not take the form of political organisations. Arab unity as propagated by Nasser was sentimentally accepted by the general public, who viewed Nasser as the leader of such a movement, and Egypt as its centre. Cairo's propaganda portrayed Egypt as the model of revolution, physical strength, industrialisation and economic progress. All these claims were shattered by Egypt's humilitating defeat in the June 1967 war. Many intellectuals came to realise that the problem of the Arabs was backwardness, which could be solved only through development in the field of science and technology, as well as in the economy and politics.[41] This brought attention to the idea of concentration on Libya as the better alternative.

The emphasis on the Libyan national identity came to the surface and found encouraging responses in various political sectors. It was sponsored by Abdul Hamid al Bakkush, a young lawyer, who was appointed prime minister on 24 October 1967.[42]

Bakkush stressed the existence of a Libyan identity which had deep roots far back in pre-history, and emphasised the integrity and unity which the Libyan people had been able to preserve throughout their long history. He pointed to the "new society" in which the Libyans adhered to their land, felt their identity, and worked for the welfare of all. He stressed that whatever role Libya could play would be more effective when it came from a self-confident and fully independent Libya.[43] However, the fall of Bakkush from power on 4 September 1968 was a setback for the idea of the Libyan national identity, but it was in no way to mark its end, since the change was in itself a reflection of the wishes and aspirations of a large segment of the Libyan people.

CONCLUSION

The evaluation of the Libyan political system during the period 1952-1969 reflected features of both continuity and change. The socio-economic realities of three entities with their own regional particularisms, different backgrounds and distinct interests led to the adoption of the federal system as a stop-gap before complete unification would be gradually achieved. However, the process of social integration was much faster than expected, and thus, within a decade through a mixture of population, joint collaboration, education and political orientation, the process of Libyanisation prevailed over any provincial attachment. The decision for unification was taken unanimously in Parliament, and in the legislatures of the provinces, and was implemented in two stages, the abrogation of the political status of the provinces, and later the abrogation of their administative status in favour of *Muhafadhah* governates.

The policies of the state were conducted by King Idris indirectly through various organs of governemnt. Neither organised opposition nor free press were allowed and the political institutions were reduced to mere instruments of policy. The whole of domestic politics was performed by balancing the power of various elements of the government and by the manipulation of various leading pesonalities, through frequent changes of cabinets, continuous reshuffles, and control of parliamentary elections. However, towards the end of the first decade, with the spread of education and the returns form oil, new men came to the forefront aspiring to

Political developments 1952-1969

political status. King Idris was flexible enough to draw some of his supporters from among their ranks, and appealed to the masses from time to time through appointments of benevolent cabinets sensitive to their wishes and aspirations.

Internationally, he avoided any direct political involvement, despite his unquestioned pro-Western policy, of which the existence of Western military bases were living evidence. His insistence on keeping the military bases and the way in which he manipulated the political institutions raised the question of the credibility of the whole system, and led to its eventual downfall.

The ideology of the regime emerged from the first years of independence. It centred around independence, unity, and King Idris as a national symbol. Through this simple ideology the process of Libyanisation, which led to eventual unification, was successfully carried out. By the 1960s changes at international, regional and national levels created a completely different atmosphere. New men with new outlooks, new philosophies and new ideas emerged. Some of them were involved in political movements and the political parties of the areas. Others were for Arab unity or for special concentration on Libya, without having any organised political status. The fall of the political parties in the areas as a result of their June 1967 war, paved the way for the idea of concentration on Libya which was revived, reactivated, and presented in "the Libyan national identity" of Abdul Hamid al Bakkush. The fall of Bakkush from power constituted a setback to the idea, and the fall of the regime as a whole only a few months later brought in a completely different system of leadership, government and ideology which falls outside the scope of this chapter.

Notes

1. Khadduri, M., *Modern Libya*, Baltimore, The Johns Hopkins Press, 1963, pp 10910 and pp 141-179
2. The Admirate of Cyrenaica, *Al Jarida al Rasmiyya* (The Official Gazette) cited hereafter as JR Lib, Circular No 187, No 3-12, 11 October 1950, pp 13-20; Ibid, Circular No 188, p 21; and Ibid, No 3, 14 January 1950, pp 1-2
3. Khadduri, *op. cit.*, pp 107-109
4. On party politics in Tripolitania see Zyada, N., *Libya fi Sanat 1948, Wathika Rasmiyya* (Libya in 1949, an Official Document), Beirut, The American

University Publications, 1966. See also Shunayti M., *Kadiyyat Libya* (The Libyan Case), Cairo, Al Nahda al Misiyya Book Co, 1951, pp 276-48

5. Khadduri, *op. cit.*, pp 168-69
6. For more details see Pelt, A., *Libyan Independence and the United Nations*, Newhaven, Yale University Press, 1970, pp 299 onwards
7. The People's Court Proceedings, the Royal Household Trial, 23 October - 16 November 1971, Trial of the Ex-Crown Prince, 24-25 October 1971, and the trial of Wanis al Gaddafi, and ex Prime Minister, 30 October 1971
8. Muhammad al Tayyid al Ashhab,*Ibrahim al Shalhi*, Cairo, Mukhaimir Press, 1956, p43. See also The People's Court Proceedings, The Royal Household Trial, *op. cit.*,The Trial of the Ex-Crown Prince, 23 October 1971
9. The Libyan Constitution, Article 86
10. Ibid., Articles 36 and 38
11. Ibid., Articles 179, 181, 182 and 183
12. The People's Court Proceedings: the 1952 Elections, the trials of Fadil bin Zikri,and ex-governor, Mahmud al Khoja, an ex Mutasarrif, Abdullah bin Sha'aban, an ex-Kaimmakam, and Ahmad Rifat, an ex-police officer, 1 August 1971; ibid., The Royal Household Trial, Abdul Aziz al Shali, testimony, and testimony of Nuri Siddigh Ismail, the ex-chief of staff of the Libyan Armed Forces, 23 October-16 November 1971
13. Mohammad al Tayyid al Ashhab, *Libya al Yawm* (Libya Today), Baghdad, Al as'ad Press, 1955, p 36; the United Kingdom of Libya, *Al Jarida al Rasmiyya JR Lib*, VI, 18 July 1955, p 2; ibid., 28 June 1956, p 21
14. The Sanusi Zawiyas were abolished in November 1970, and their employees were transferred to other jobs in the bureaucracy; see *Al Raid* (newspaper), 26 November 1970
15. Khadduri, *op. cit.*, pp 240-43
16. Ibid., pp 320-22
17. *JR Lib*, Special Issue, 8 December 1962, pp 4-5
18. Ibid., 27 April 1963, p 3
19. The reactivated Sanusi institutions provided political positions for some politicians of religious background whose traditional education would not qualify them to fite in active modern institutions.
20. *al Zaman* (newspaper), 27 January 1955; see also Khadduri, *op. cit., pp 249-52*
21. Shortly after the assassination of Ibrahim

al Shalhi, Kind Idris moved to the distant and isolated area of Tubruq, where he remained unti his final departure

22. The People's Court Proceedings, the 1952 Elections: The Trial of the ex-Wali Fadil bin Zikri, 1 August 1971

23. Ibid., The Newsmen Trial, 17 January 1972- 2 March 1972

24. Statistics drawn by the author from *JR Lib*, through the period 1952-1969

25. The People's Court Proceedings: The 1952 Elections - 1 August 1971

26. Ibid., the 1956 elections, trials of Bishti, an ex-head of a provincial executive council; Bin Halim, an ex-prime minister; and Souf, an ex-Nazir (provincial minister); and the testimony of Ali al Dib, an ex-controversial politician, 20-23 October 1971

26. *JR Lib*, XV, 15 October 1961, p 12

27. The People's Court Proceedings, the 1964 and the 1965 elections, the trials of Ibrahim bin Sha'aban, ex-deputy prime minister, Bishti and Fadil al Amir, ex-ministers, 25 August 1971; and the testimonies of candidates who were arrested, among them Zummit, Lakhdar, and al Misrati, 30 August 1971; also the testimonies of the policement who received orders from their superiors to break into the ballot boxes, among them Hamza, Ghazzi, Gliyya, etc 5 September 1971

28. *JR Lib*, VIII, 25 April 1963, p5

29. On Fkeni's policies, visits, activities, and statements see the newspapers of *Tarabulus al Gharb*, 8 July 1963, 28-30 August 1963, and 1 January 1964; and *Al Raid*, 1 January and 1 February 1964. See also Sami Hakim, *Hadhili Libya* (This is Libya), Cairo, The Anglo-Egyptian Book Company, 1970, pp 73-96

30. *JR Lib*, III, 10 March 1964, p 11; ibid., III, 3 October 1964, p 11; ibid., XII, 6 April 1967, p 14

31. The Bakkush Reform Programme gained wide publicity and he was able to mobilise a large segment of young graduates for its implementation; see about it, *JR Lib*, III, (15 December 1967), p 3 and ibid., II, 12 January 1968, pp 6-7; *The Libyan Review*, III, 8 August 1968, pp 13-16; *Libya al Haditha* (Modern Libya) (a magazine), 18 February 1969; *Tarabulus al Gharb*, 20 November 1968, and *al 'Alam*, 2 July 1968

32. *Al Raid*, 4 February 1964, for a summary of Nasser's speech and text of Muntasir's announce-

ment, and ibid., 16 March 1964, for the news of the Parliament's unanimous vote to end the agreements directing the government to negotiate for these ends

33. His insistence that the military bases should continue was made clear to Ben Halim in the aftermath of the Suez crisis, to Fkeni when he proposed their liquidation in 1963. and to Muntasir in 1964, he even pleaded ill-health and threatened to resign. See respectively Khadduri *op. cit.*, p 298, the People's Court Proceedings: The Royal Household Trial, Fkeni testimony, 3 November 1971, and *Al Raid*, 23 March 1964, for the King's explanation of resignation and its withdrawal

34. The King's statement was propagated as one of his wise sayings, and spread as a slogan everywhere. Se also Khadduri, *op. cit.*, p 320

35. Ibid., pp 320-22

36. Abdullah al Eweri, Ma'ana al Kiyan (The meaning of identity), Beirut, Dar'lubnan Press, n.d.

37. On the development of this movement see Ishak Musa al Husaini, *The Moslem Brethern*, Beirut, Khayat's, 1956

38. Khadduri, *op. cit.*, p 331

39. See *JR Trip*, Special Issue, 13 December 1961, pp 2-9, list of the Ba'athists arrested; see also Hakim, *Hadhihi Libya, op.cit.*, pp 195-97; and *JR Lib*, XIV, 25 December 1964, p 23, for the newspaper suspension

40. See *Al'Alam*, 2 February 1968, for the prosecutor's statement in court; see also Hakim, *Hadhihi Libya, op. cit.*, pp 229-44

41. See for example Sadik al Azay, *Al Nakd al Dhati B'ada al Hazima* (Self-criticism after the Defeat), Beirut, Dar al Tali'a, 1968; and Constanin Zuraik, *Ma'ana al Nakha Mujaddadan*(The meaning of the disaster renewed), Beirut, Dar al Tali'a, 1968

42. Bakkush was a leftist while he was a student in Cairo. He changed his views later and switched to the idea of a special concentration on Libya

43. Ministry of Information and Culture, *The Bakkush Speech of 21 November 1964 on the anniversary of the United Nations Resolution on Libyan Independence*, Tripoli, The Government Press, 1967, pp 1-22; and *The Libyan Review*, III, 8 August 1968, pp 13-16

Political Developments 1952-1969

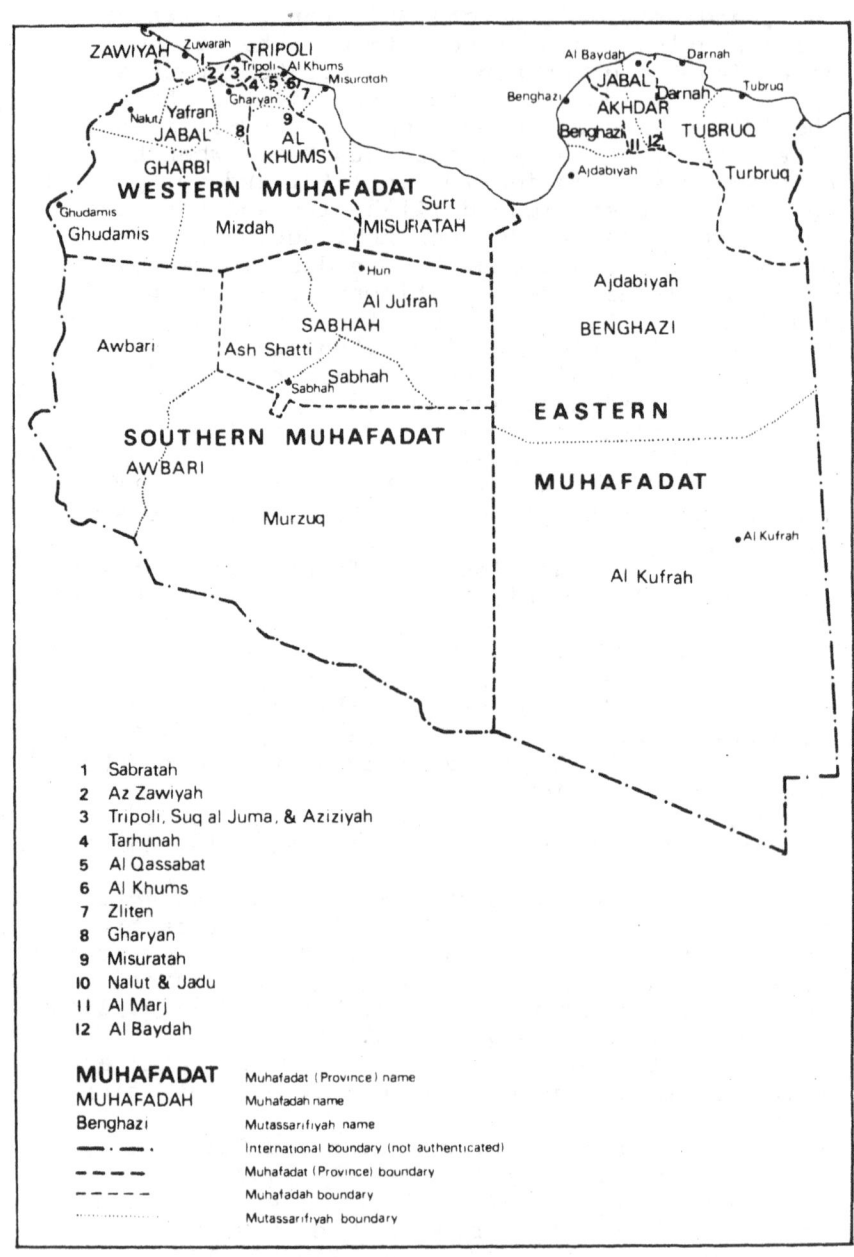

Figure 7. Administrative Divisions of Libya pre-1969

Chapter 10
THE GREEN BOOK: ITS CONTEXT AND MEANING

Hervé Bleuchot

INTRODUCTION

Colonel Mu^{c}ammar Qadhafi's views are little known by the outside world and, when discussed, are usually distorted and rarely given serious and disinterested consideration. The Western press treats him with caricature and superficiality, usually as the result of a limited number of interviews by journalists who do not have an adequate knowledge either of Libya or of Arabic. Like all politicians, Colonel Qadhafi is skilled in the political art of evasiveness and, as a result, it becomes impossible for such journalists to interpret his declarations correctly. The situation has noticeable improved since the Jamahiriya Arab News Agency (JANA) started publishing a daily bulletin in French. However, the least that can be said of this bulletin is that it is far from satisfactory. For example, in a speech on 1 September 1980, Colonel Qadhafi proposed union between Libya and Syria, yet the JANA bulletin made no mention of this important event.

Yet it would also be inadequate to rely solely on *The Green Book* as a guide to Colonel Qadhafi's thoughts, for this is merely a transitory stage in the Colonel's intellectual development which is actually richer and more diversified in its daily vitality than a simple example of its expression can possibly show.[1]

Can we actually comprehend Colonel Qadhafi's thought? In fact the task is relatively easy because, fortunately, Colonel Qadhafi is a frequent and extensive speaker. It is as if he believes that he should repeatedly recapitulate what he has said in order to make it clearer and more explicit. In his numerous speeches, as he dwells on the same themes in different terms, he argues that one particular speech should be corrected by another. The numerous seminars he called were designed not so much to gain celebrity as to incite intellectuals to express their intuitions in the best possible ways. Indeed, Colonel Qadhafi resents flattery as much as he does malevolent criticism, for he is looking for collaboration between intellectuals both in Libya and elsewhere. When some of his over-zealous friends attempt to spare him criticism, they cause great harm to Qadhafi, Libya and to democracy.

While reading the proceedings of the Benghazi Seminar held in October 1979 I was struck by two different attitudes adopted towards Qadhafi's philosophy. The first, which clearly required considerable courage to express, consists of a global rejection of everything without considering Qadhafi's ideological motivations. The second attitude simply accepts the vision of the leader of Libya's revolution and tries to develop some simple aspect alone. I would like to propose a third approach which, starting from the Colonel's expressed views, analyses his motivations, the influences on him and his reasoning. We will then go beyond what he actually says to explore what he really wants to say - often far richer and anchored deeply in human experience. The questions that arise cannot be answered with a simple yes or no, but only through terms such as why, how and maybe. Qadhafi's vision is a scientific one, and worthy of serious consideration; it is not just an expression of a political attitude. We must, then, look at the Libyan context: the exercise of power there, the political classes that exist in Libya, and international problems.

We can identify several stages in the development of Qadhafi's thought, not always distinct from one another, as evidence of the constant evolution which it has undergone. The first period runs from 1 September 1969 (the date of the Revolution) to the beginning of 1973. Then, from the Zuwarah speech which inaugurated the Cultural Revolution until 1976, we are dealing with a transitional period in which we can already discern the themes of the *The Green Book*. During this period Qadhafi's thought was basically dominated by Nasserist influences, particularly in respect to international relations. Finally, there is the second period which began in 1977 with the appearance of three volumes of *The Green Book*. This period, which was really a reflection of Qadhafi's own views for the first time, saw the emergence of his ideas on Islam.[2] However, depending on circumstances, older themes

The Green Book: its context and meaning

can still reappear throughout it.

THE FIRST PERIOD: QADHAFI THE NASSERIST

Colonel Qadhafi's ideology began to develop during the previous regime of King Idris. A quick survey of the political and social situation during this period will be necessary to put this in context.

The old regime and the young Qadhafi

The old king Idris As-Sanussi, who reigned over Libya from 1951 to 1969, was never able to rid himself completely of a mentality which characterised the post-War period. He remained loyal to his Anglo-Saxon allies who had helped to drive out Libya's Italian colonisers. These allies had provided him with significant aid in return for important political concessions, particularly the granting of military bases at Wheelus Field and Tubruq. He was unable to appreciate the new situation for the Arab world, with the Palestine conflict, or the Nasserist phenomenon and its influence.
    The discovery of important oil fields and their initial exploitation led to Libyan dependence on the Anglo-Saxon oil companies which were to be responsible for the introduction of a capitalist economy into the country. Libyan tribal society, already seriously shaken by the Italian presence from 1912 to 1942, although temporarily reconstituted during the British occupation from 1942 to 1951, apparently provided a reliable base for the religious regime of Idris, who was himself head of a religious order. The introduction of a monetary economy seriously undermined tribal society, for nothing could have been more fatal to traditional relations based on religious prestige and tribal or religious authority than money earned by oil workers, who had previously been the docile sons of their Sanussi fathers and who had been kept contemptuously at the social margin. Newly accumulated fortunes gave rise to another kind of prestige, based on the Mercedes, a villa in Tripoli, and travel to Europe or the United States. Tribal society lost its primitive roughness and its cohesion to the head of the Sanussi order - King Idris. He soon began to appear as an accomplice of the West and therefore of Israel, and as a protector of a newly enriched minority which monopolised revenues drawn from the oil companies.

The Green Book: its context and meaning

A new social class - the middle class - began to appear. Civil servants, policemen, soldiers and teachers were needed. Import trade created an important merchant class. The peasantry, on the other hand, began to die out with the departure of the Italians and Libyan agriculture came to an effective stop. Social outcasts became numerous and included migrant peasants, the unemployed in the shanty towns, and nomad stock raisers who lacked resources. On top of all these problems was a political one, for political parties were not allowed, and foreigners, even the Italians, seemed in charge everywhere.

The future Colonel Qadhafi was born in 1941 into a tribe of the Gulf of Surt, so he started life with a name, a father, and a tribe at least. As a youth, he listened to "The Voice of the Arabs", and dreamt of an Arab nation which would be strong and great at a time when the radio told him that it was divided, dominated and demoralised. It was divided because it had been colonised by the West and the numerous political parties only added to this division. It was dominated because it did not use its own language, its oil was under-priced and foreigners were the real masters who exploited reactionary Arab governments as their agents. The Arab nation was demoralised because it was humiliated by the numerous defeats it had suffered at the hands of the colonisers, the Jewish state, and from the self-inflicted wounds that resulted from failures at attempts at unity, as well as the war in the Yemen. For Qadhafi the situation in Libya was worst of all, for King Idris was nothing more than a puppet in the hands of his entourage; Libya was still one of the few African countries to have foreign military bases on its soil and, even worse, Israeli planes which attacked Egypt in 1967 had come from the West. Last but not least, Libyan parliamentary democracy was just a fake based on rigged elections.

Such attitudes over the situation in Libya were shared by almost everybody there and, when Colonel Qadhafi took power in 1969 he raised immense hopes which were manifested by continuous demonstrations. Qadhafi had faith in the people and expressed their frustrations - everybody wanted Arab unity but it always failed to materialise. Why? Because of conservative governments... Within the tribe people used to share property and costs, fortune and misfortune. Why then look for a model of democracy elsewhere? The obstacle was created by puppet governments controlled by foreigners. Moreover, Arabs and Libyans, despite their oil, were still poor. Why? Because they were being robbed. Libya and the Muslim world seemed to be God's forgotten subjects. God, however, cannot forget Muslims. Thus these must have betrayed their religion, a religion which is inherently revolutionary, simple and egalitarian.

Arabism and Islam

With these simple ideas, profoundly anchored in popular Arab mental attitudes, Qadhafi came to power on 1 September 1969. Initially he had nothing new to propose in the institutional field, and the provisional constitution of 11 December 1969 was just a copy of the Egyptian constitution. A single political party was created, the Arab Socialist Union, with the same name and almost the same goals as its Egyptian counterpart. Political practice until 1973 clearly showed a determination to avoid intermediaries and an evident desire to turn to direct popular power through popular meetings in which the ordinary man could make direct contact with the head of state, the members of the Revolutionary Command Council (RCC) or the Ministers.[3]

Until the death of Colonel Nasser in September 1970, Colonel Qadhafi constantly repeated the same themes as his intellectual master.[4] The slogan of the Libyan Arab Republic at that time was, "liberty, socialism, unity", the same as Egypt. Yet, even then, there was already a particular emphasis on Islamic themes. Qadhafi began to appear as the champion of Islam, initially by not being ashamed of reaffirming his attachment to it, then by prohibiting the sale of alcholic drinks in Libya, and finally by encouraging Islamic missionary activity in Africa.

Yet he did not belong to the Muslim Brotherhood. He distinguished himself from it very early on because the Brotherhood did not believe in Arab nationalism. On 30 August 1972 he declared, "Some newspapers write that those who govern the Arab Republic of Libya are Muslim Brothers and not revolutionaries, as if a Muslim should necessarily belong to the Muslim Brotherhood and a progressive necessarily be a communist". The Colonel's ultimate aim was to devise a third way which reconciled religion and progressivism. During this period he frequently turned to practising Muslims, rejecting fanaticism and seeking dialogue, particularly in 1973.

Nevertheless, the main principle of Qadhafi's ideology was still Arabism. The relationship between this ideology and Islam and *The Green Book* can best be understood by analysing it in terms of the concept *umma* (religious community or nation). It is a concept which is specific to Islam, for the *umma* comprises the community of the believers, the community of the prophet *(ummat al-nabi)*.[5] Gardet has observed that this community of believers has always wanted to become a single state or a group of strong states (p285). He also argues that Arabism does not pose a threat to the *umma* of believers, because "Arabism involves Islamic values, the reformist dream of an Islamic restoration."

It is in this sense that Colonel Qadhafi envisaged the *umma*. During this period, the *umma* was always an *umma ^{c}arabiya*, because Islam had no meaning without the Arabs. "The Arab nation gives Islam the weight it has" (16/9/69). His opposition to the Muslim Brotherhood was a logical consequence, because they saw Islam as primary whether Arabs were involved or not. Qadhafi's response was to say that "the Muslim Brotherhood movement is at present a natural extension of the *shu^{c}ubiya*[6], movements which deeply resent the *umma ^{c}arabiya* and Arab nationalism.. as if there were a contradiction between Arab nationalism and the teaching of Islam" (7/5/73). To justify his views the Colonel resorted to the Quran and quoting the well-known verse "Ye are the best community that hath been raised up to mankind" (3,110), explaining that "nobody should interpret this verse as including all Muslims" (16/09/73). He claims that it applied only to the Arabs.

The religious meaning of *umma* is thus reduced to the concept of Arabism as nationalism. The Colonel's aim is clearly to restore the Arab greatness before anything else. "Arab unity is the first and most important step towards Islamic unity" (24/01/71). However, when he states that "We do not need an Islamic party" (24/01/71), the question arises as to whether Islamic unity figures amongst his objectives. In fact Qadhafi puts Islam - the Quran - to the service of Arabism. He quotes another well-known verse, "And hold fast all together, to the cable of Allah, and do not separate from each other" (3,103). In a speech on 1 September 1971, he emphasised that this verse was addressed to the Arabs, particularly to the citizens of Libya, Egypt and Syria, who that day were to vote in a referendum to establish an Arab Federation. For Qadhafi the vote was part of a sacred march *(al-zahf al-muqaddas)* towards the re-emergence of the Arab nation and the liberation of Palestine.

Yet, besides Islam, we often come across references to universal values in the Colonel's thought, such as liberty, humanism, peace, for his ambition, in the highest sense of the word, is universal too. This Arab orientation in the philosophy of the leader of the Libyan revolution has led to a series of setbacks. There was first the failure of union with Egypt, Syria and the Sudan, then of union with Egypt and Syria, and finally the abortive attempt at unity with Egypt in 1973 and with Tunisia in 1974, as well as other lesser known attempts at union with the Sudan and Algeria, amongst others. There were also other, more secret, failures on the Arab front, paricularly in Lebanon. Colonel Qadhafi was so deeply disappointed with the Arab world that he then turned to Africa, but as Africans are not Arabs, the concept of *umma arabiya* necessarily changed. In *The Green Book*, for instance, the concept of *umma* is not defined, - it is neither Arab nor Islamic.

Socialism and Islam

First we must clarify what is meant by the concept of socialism for Colonel Qadhafi. The Colonel discusses socialism quite often, but gives it various definitions. Certainly, socialism must be clearly distinguished from Marxism and communism, which are nothing but forms of atheist socialism. Authentic socialism is to be found in Islam "The Islamic religion is certainly more progressive than communism. It laid the foundations of the economic system, relations between workers, the conditions for a society of abundance, self-sufficiency *(kifaya)*, justice and freedom. Let everyone know that Islam manifested these ideas long before Marx and Lenin. Islam is clearly an eternal message, a continuous revolution, a new ideology and the mother of all theory" (12/12/70). "... Today, I declare that the Arab nation is honoured by being the precursor of socialism, since socialist principles are found in the Quran. Neither Marx nor Lenin, nor other theoreticians and philosophers have succeeded in devising a better system than Islam in the economic, social and moral fields" (01/09/71).

These two questions make it clear that Qadhafi draws his ideas both from Islam and contemporary

The Green Book: its context and meaning

Bedouin society. *The Green Book* is also based on these two sources. As early as 16 September 1969 the Colonel stated that "Socialism means participating in production. It is the achievement of self-sufficiency *(kifaya)* in production without exploitation, theft, illegality or the violation of religious prohibitions *(bi ghayri haram)* and without usury or bribery". All these ideas were to reappear in *The Green Book*, under a less religious cover.

During this period, commentators tended to draw parallels between this concept of socialism and Nasserist Islamic socialism. In fact it is basically a capitalist system in which social consequences are controlled. The main profile of socialism in Libya until the 1977/1978 period involved a redistribution of income through graduated taxation and social security, worker participation in management and profits, a controlled price system, particularly for basic foodstuffs, free or very cheap distribuiton of land and housing. The Islamic aspect of an economic system like this is practically non-existent. The public *awqaf* (pious endowments), which could be considered to be a socialist institution based on Islam (since the *awqaf* were used to maintain, *inter alia*, the poor, students, hospitals and asylums) were not seen as a basis for Islamic socialist society. In Libya, as elsewhere in the Muslim world, *awqaf* have been reduced in importance and marginalised. The introduction of Islamic law, on theft and adultery, given much publicity at the time, did not alter the logic of the Western-inspired Libyan judicial system.[7]

The importance of power in practice and the development of *The Green Book*

It has been suggested that Colonel Qadhafi had raised immense hopes and enjoyed popular support. The upper class of the old regime, consisting of a privileged minority, had lost all influence and had vanished as a social group. Some were imprisoned, others left the country. The middle class, which formed the majority of the urban population, supported the new regime. However, this support was based on a degree of misunderstanding. The group in question wanted a pro-Arab policy, solidarity with the Arab world against Israel, good relations with neighbouring countries and a non-aligned foreign policy, but did not want adventure either in international or internal politics. Internally, it was in favour of a rapid industrialistation, flourishing trade, a solid infrastructure and efficient administration. It would have preferred to see oil revenues contribute to the building of an economy capable of surviving when the oilfields would run dry. In other words, it wanted to be governed by a Boumedienne and, of course, did not find the man it was looking for in Qadhafi. Egocentric Libyan nationalism is totally incompatible with Qadhafi's mentality and very early on he realised the nature of the opposition that faced him.

In September 1971 he even offered his resignation. In a speech at Sabratah he explained his reasons, "It is the incompetence of the administration which paralyses all social, economic and industrial plans. To protest against this state of things, which is something I cannot understand, I offer my resignation... What we want to do as a priority is to change everything" (4/10/71). Despite an administrative reform in 1972, nothing really changed. Qadhafi realised that Nasserist ideas had merely led to a society lacking in originality which was revolutionary and socialist only in words and slogans. It is this that explains his Zuwarah speech in 1973 and the popular Cultural Revolution that succeeded it (15/04/73).

The themes and the aspect of this Revolution have been described in detail elsewhere (see note 3), and need not detain us again. What should be kept in mind is that the following pattern was constantly repeated - faced with opposition the Colonel incited the masses *(jamahir)* through a speech to overcome the obstacles that faced it. The Revolution was not be to achieved by decree but through the masses who were to launch an assault *(zahf)* on the institutions of government. Qadhafi attempted to use this tactic against Sadat in 1973 when the latter was reluctant to accept union between Egypt and Libya. However, the attempt to achieve unity through a popular march *(zahf)* failed on this occasion, because the Egyptian people were not ready to support it. Yet, every popular action has resulted in the creation of a new opposition to it, thus causing a perpetual movement forwards and a permanent Revolution directed by speeches and executed by the people. However, one may ask, which people? Not the middle classes, but the lower strata - minor civil servants, employees, workers, dockers, and the jobless.

The various stages of this movement have been described elsewhere. Its results consisted of the abolition of the Arab Socialist Union, the embodiment of the middle classes' aspirations, which claimed to control the popular committee revolution in 1973. These committees were in turn replaced by a system of popular congresses described in *The Green Book*, Vol 1 which discusses direct democracy, because its principles were in fact applied before it was written. Amongst these principles were the abolition of the Revolutionary Command Council (RCC) the majority of whose members in August 1975 attempted to reject Colonel Qadhafi and which no longer corresponded to the concept of direct democracy, and the forcing of students into line in April 1976 after hostile demonstrations. *The Green Book* appeared at the end of 1976, at a time when the system it described was already functioning. The proclamation of "Popular Power" in March 1977 was a mere formality, and with the official change of name from the "Libyan Arab Republic" to "Socialist People's Libyan Arab Jamahiriya", Libya became the "state of the masses".

The second volume of *The Green Book* appeared at the beginning of 1978 and was followed in 1979 by the third volume. The application of the principles enunciated in these books began with their publication as well, and it is to them that we now turn.

CRITICAL INTERPRETATION AND REFLECTIONS ON THE GREEN BOOK

General interpretation

Volume 3 of *The Green Book* exemplifies the basic ideas underlying the whole work. It apparently begins with the curious concept of social links being assimilated into national bonds. In fact this confusion is due to the Arabic language in which the term *qawmiya* (Nationalism) is derived from the word *qawm* (tribe), which has taken over the meaning of nation only recently, since the beginning of the 20th century. Colonel Qadhafi is not a sociologist and the jargon associated with this discipline is beyond his competence. In his writings he uses concepts generally available to him - family, tribe and Arabism, for example. However, his speeches show that his concept of *umma* and of social relations, as we shall see in the third part of this paper, are rather different.

The task of the translator who had to render the third volume of *The Green Book* into other languages was not easy, and it has proved extremely difficult to capture the conceptual complexities of the original Arabic.

The Green Book: its context and meaning

These problems were resolved basically by using different translations for the term *qawm* 'nation' and 'community', and *jama^{c}a* as 'group' or 'society'. Thus from *jama^{c}a* (group), it was possible to move to *qawmiya* (nationalism), a word derived from *qawm*. In this way the chain of meaning was maintained complete.

In fact Qadhafi wanted to find a theoretical justification of the idea that the only authentic natural social link was one of blood. An individual was linked to others firstly by the family and then the tribe was simply an enlarged family and the nation - now seen as a 'natural' society - was a group of tribes. The result of this reasoning was to legitimise traditional Bedouin society.

For Qadhafi, then, society is based on a natural model. Individuals without family are merely vagabonds *(sa^{c}alik)*. The idea stems from an idealistic vision of early Islam when pre-Islamic vagabondage was much despised. In any case, the Bedouin ideal has always been present in Arab thought. In 1930 the poet Ahmad Chawqi praised the Queen Dowager of Egypt, describing her luxurious car or carriage as a "palanquin", its door as a "veil" and its steering wheel as "reins".[8] Poets were not alone in taking Bedouin society as a model. The "least Arab of the Arabs" as Bourguiba, at that time a lawyer, used to be described, entered Tunis in 1955 on horseback wearing Bedouin dress. The period of the Rightly Guided Caliphs *(al-khulafa' al-rashidun)* was always considered as a golden age, not only for religious reasons but also because it was a period in which the individual, freely backed by his tribe, and strong in the support of his sword and family, could defy the world. The young Qadhafi grew up in a social milieu where ties of blood and religion were stronger than any other social link. In his speeches he has mentioned how, during his youth, he was fascinated by the word "Arab". "The first thing that impressed us was the knowledge that we were Arabs. It is the word 'Arab' that is most often heard in the tribe" (25/06/70). Equally the worst insult that could be addressed to former King Idris was the fact that he was a 'vagabond... He did not belong to the Libyan people; he was a merchant, a courtier..." (17/06/75).

It is this way that the third volume of *The Green Book* clarifies the ideas behind the first two volumes. Direct democracy is true democracy because it it an institution in which, from the earliest times, the individual would come armed to

an assembly. Indeed the theme of a people in arms
is an important one in Qadhafi's ideology: in Libya
arms have been distributed to the tribe but not to
the "vagabonds" - foreigners, immigrants and rootless
people.[9] There was no need to look elsewhere for a
democratic model and, in any case, the young Qadhafi
had no knowledge of the outside world. All that he
knew of the West was tainted by brutality, through
colonialism and fascism, cupidity, through capitalism
and commercial greed, or immorality, through films
and pornography. What he knew of socialism was no
more inviting - atheism and dictatorship, for example.
The only valid model for him was his own warm envelop-
ing democratic egalitarian and austere society.

Volume 2 of *The Green Book* also becomes clear when
considered in the light of the Bedouin ideal. Wage-
earning classes were unknown in the tribe. They were
confined only to vagabonds, servants and other in-
ferior individuals. Life in the tribe was based on
free association, and distribution depended on the
principle "to each according to his needs and no
more". Economic accumulation within the tribe was
unknown because there was no need for it. The land
belonged to everybody, it was only pasture for use
by nomads.[10] To divide it up would be as meaningless
as trying to divide fresh air and sunshine. Custom
regulated all aspects of life as natural law and
complex legislation, such a labour law, commercial
law or constitutions, had no relevance to tribal
society. Ottoman legislation of the *Tanzimat* period,
just like Italian legislation, was to have no
tangible effect on Libyan society.

The third volume of *The Green Book* is also full
of eulogies to this kind of life. Thus the tribe
is perceived as an educational institution which
confers upon the individual "a more complete and
noble social education than any academic instruc-
tion" (III, 15). It is views like this that explain
Qadhafi's rejection of ideas like nurseries for
children. The child should stay with its family.
"It is against nature to separate children from their
mothers" (III, 30). A child who has no family is
like a rootless vagabond. It would be abandoned in
a natural society, but in such a case Libya would
have to be generous by providing appropriate
institutions (III, 29). Modern industrial societies
are considered to be "uncivilised... just materialist
societies" (III, 36). For Qadhafi the evidence for
these concepts is undeniable.

His views on sports and entertainment might seem
very odd at first sight. "(Sports clubs) absorb

public funds as well as the structures and equipment assigned to sport by the state. These institutions are nothing but another form of social monopoly, similar to dictatorial political instruments" (III, 53). The reasoning here seem to be that anyone who devotes himself to a specific activity necessarily monopolises it and thus excludes others from it! Sportsmen and politicians are not the only people in this situation. Doctors, mechanics and engineers also exclude others from their activity. In that case, should the masses take over operating theatres, garages and research departments? Yes, Qadhafi would answer. Yet here he is not alone, for it is also the answer given by someone such as Ivan Illich[11] - everyone should be able to treat himself, repair his car, and talk to the workers on a building site, for example. Qadhafi is also basically convinced that Bedouin austerity is incompatible with entertainment - something to which Illich also refers.[12]

The main idea behind the book is therefore a return to the natural life and to natural forms of socialism. But, how does Qadhafi in the twentieth century resolve the problems that arise from the situation that that implies? In fact such problems clearly embarrass him and some he cannot even discuss.

Direct democracy and its difficulties

The first volume of *The Green Book* is mainly dominated by what can be called the dilemma of communal democratic life. For Qadhafi, "political struggle which results in the victory of one candidate by 51 per cent of the total votes, for instance, leads to a dictatorship but under a democratic cover" (I,8). However, the problem is that there will *always* be a majority and a minority in every assembly or popular congress![13] With three persons, for example, two will oppose the one, with two, the most powerful will dominate the weaker; perfect democracy is achieved only in the absence of other people, where the individual is alone.

In fact, every authentic attempt at democracy involves protection of the individual citizen. The Swiss citizen who attends the *canton* assembly with his sword symbolises the inalienable right of the individual alone. Traditional institutions of Atlantic civilisation such as Scandinavia and Switzerland rigorously protected the individual and his political and economic independence. Yet, with Colonel Qadhafi, it seems that he proposes an ideal model without offering realistic solutions. Majorities always dominate minorities and society, which is dispersed in space, cannot meet together in one and the same place. Nor can it allow the individual to express himself without any time limit, particularly in assemblies which have no rules of debate. These problems have to be met by local meetings at the level of the constituency. Yet here society risks an even greater danger since constituency-based elections can easily lead to minority rule.[14] Opponents of parliamentary democracy have dwelt on this question at great length of course, but this conclusion is equally true even when people are divided up by territory or tribe. It is very easy to end up with a minority 45 per cent vote winning against a 55 per cent majority, something which is impossible for example in a referendum.

As far as the delegation of power is concerned, interpreted delegation certainly transfers popular power into the hands of a few individuals, and here Colonel Qadhafi's criticisms are valid. However, *The Green Book* surprisingly allows for "executive groups" which meet together in a general popular congress - something suspiciously similar to deputies in a parliament. Nonetheless, although there is a clear difference, *The Green Book* is notably brief over this matter. These executive groups are mandated by their popular congresses and may not go beyond their mandates. The general popular congress limits itself to synthesising and systematising recommendations from the popular congresses. Yet, there is still a theoretical problem for those who "control executive functions" (I,30) do not exercise power. "The control of the people by the people" (I, 31) means in reality that part of the people must stand idly by during the exercise of power, even if it can make decisions *before* and require an account *after* the event. Yet here too there is a dilemma, for Colonel Qadhafi is clearly uncertain of the system, since he writes "In practice, it is always the most powerful who govern" (I,44).

In any case, direct democracy in practice is always adversely affected by absenteeism. Studies of classical Athens show that not more than 10 or 20 per cent of the free citizens actually attended assembly meetings. The result was that a group of specialists were always present and had full knowledge of all questions under debate, while the others rarely attended and only appeared when the matters under debate directly concerned them. Frequently they could not follow the discussions either because they were illiterate or because the matters involved were so specialised and thus outside their competence. Division of labour, then, becomes inevitable. In any case, the average citizen is never able to attend trade union, political, religious, economic, cultural and sporting meetings at one and the same time. Bourgeois democracy admits this to be the case and compensates for it by providing links between "specialists" and the rest through elections. There is no such link in a system of direct democracy. All there can be are people who can attend meetings and others who cannot because the issues involved are ones of time, not of knowledge. In Bedouin society the problem is unknown, for everyone always has some time to devote to general matters since their scope is limited and involves little specialised knowledge.

In any case, in practice, democracy in a tribal milieu is difficult. What criteria will the citizen use when political parties are banned and when elections are not preceded by an electoral campaign, as is the case in Libya? The only alternative for the individual is to look to the candidate's tribal affiliations - a process which is just the opposite of democracy.[15]

Natural socialism

The second volume of *The Green Book* discusses the problem of employment in the public sector - where workers are still wage-earners. It does not come to any satisfactory conclusion, and in fact highlights the contradictions inherent in the egalitarianism on which a "natural socialist" society is based. Qadhafi writes "... their (workers') share (of revenue) will vary according to the services each offers" (II, 26). Thus skilled technicians will earn more than others because of their knowledge, although this creates a situation which the Colonel has already condemned (II, 25).

Another probem is that of savings. Citizens may only save "by reducing their own needs" (II, 25). However, "inequality in the control of wealth is not allowed" (II, 26). The logical conclusion is then one relating to inheritance. If savings can be transferred, then inequality is the natural consequence. Yet, traditional Libyan society did not recognise the right of inheritance; in some areas property was redistributed every year, thus providing a perfect balance between landed and animal capital and the population. In fact, inheritance is not discussed in the second volume of *The Green Book*, although it was guaranteed by Article 8 of the Provincial Constitution of 11 December 1969.

A final issue raised in the second volume of *The Green Book* concerned the concept of legislation. For Qadhafi, only custom is a valid form of legislation and, apparently, does not contradict religion (I, 34ff). Positive law, as formulated by man, is unable, he claims, to meet man's needs (II, 28). Nevertheless, it is the only way in which problems involving workers, for instance, can be settled (II, 31). Once again the difficulty of applying the "natural" model of Bedouin society to our complex societies appears.

In the third volume of *The Green Book*, Qadhafi also finds difficulties in providing satisfactory answers to questions dealing with modern life. For instance, he offers no solution to the problems of whether women should work or not. On the one hand, the Colonel wants to protect a woman's freedom and to allow for the family to have a supplementary source of income: yet, on the other hand, he wants children brought up at home and women spared being brutalised by work which might affect their very nature. Wealthy Western society solves this through part-time work and in Libya, it seems, women are to be encouraged to become teachers. Nonetheless, the third volume of *The Green Book* does not propose any theoretical solution to this contradiction.

Education is another field full of contradictions. "Society should provide the young with all kinds of educational activities and allow them to choose freely the discipline they wish to study" (II(, 44). Obviously, not everybody can undertake literary studies for professions such as accountants, doctors and soldiers are bound to be needed. In reality, of course, Libya has not been able to avoid orientating youth over the past ten years towards disciplines that correspond to social need. Although youth in the West is certainly coerced by the fear of unemployment and the attractions of high salaries towards particular types of activity, in practice they have more freedom of choice than in Libya.

The philosophical concept of "nation"

Volume 3 of *The Green Book* contains a rephrasing of Renan's famous definition - "ultimately the nation is a feeling of belonging together and sharing of a common destiny" (III, 9). Renan had actually written "A nation is a soul and a spirit ... sharing common glories in the past and a common will in the present".

The leader of the Libyan Revolution does not seem to be aware that this definition first emerged in a different milieu and in response to quite different circumstances. It was created only after it had become evident that it was not blood, religion or land alone that constituted a nation, for such an entitiy could only be defined by a desire for communal life. Each of these concepts had represented a step in a long historical process. The French Revolution rejected royal absolutism and legal discrimination based on social origin. Earlier improvements had involved the rejection of religious law which forced the individual conscience to accept the state's religion. Another improvement was the disappearance of kinship-based law - the oldest type of discrimination, easily used to justify individual slavery or death. The *jus sanguinis* also underlay many other forms of discrimination, of which the most obvious was racism. Such improvements are mainly due to the struggles of marginal and rejected social elements who have wished to be included within the nation - amongst them for instance Huguenots, papists, Jews, serfs, the Third Estate, refugees and blacks. Renan's concept of nation was the ultimate formula which accepted all groups without distinction. Modern Western society is now prepared to accept and naturalise groups such as blacks, Asiatics, Muslims and Buddhists, the rich and the poor, and even people without country, tribe or family. Its aim is to overcome its old internal conflicts by reducing all specific minorities to a single concept of citizenship as defined by the Human Rights Declaration. The individual is then related to other entities (family, club, political party, church or nation) only by his willingness to live in common with them. In other words, he lives with them by his own free choice. He would be greatly disadvantaged if he were formally identified by race, as in Nazi Germany for instance, religion or political creed. After all, the ideal of the open society is that it should be open to all, whether stateless exiles, persecuted persons or even vagabonds.

It is certainly the case that Renan's ideal nation is far from being realised in the West, because the survival of racism, the rejection of minorities, class discrimination, foreign exploitation and discrimination of all sorts still exist. Alternatives such as socialist society have attempted to do away with the power of capital and even the concept of nation itself in order to establish the supremacy of humanity. Depite these ideals, however, such society has met with many obstacles, amongst them national, religious, political and racial factors, without being able to preserve the liberty acquired by the French Revolution.

Colonel Qadhafi does not seem to be completely aware of these considerations. When discussing modern nations he observes that they have been undermined by minorities, which shows that kinship is still the natural basis of nationalism.[16] He also argues that there are nations whose components are welded together with religion - the Arab nation being one example. However, even these empires are breaking down and the only possible viable basis, therefore, is one of common origin. Qadhafi admits that "the ideal would be a situation in which each nation has its own religion" (III, 9), and regrets the loss of original social harmony whereby "each community had its religion" (III, 9).

In short, Mu^{c}ammar Qadhafi is not so interested by what a nation is as by what it should be - a community sharing ties of blood, religion, land and law. The desire for communal life, then, is a result of these factors and not the sole requirement necessary for nationhood. The answer again lies in Qadhafi's social experience when he was young. In the Maghreb there are no Christian or Jewish Arabs. "Christian" or "Jew" then simply meant "foreigner", and thus a potential enemy. He has never admitted, for example, that Berbers might not be of Arab origin. In a recent interview with the Beirut newspaper *al-Safir* he declared that "Arab Christians should adopt Islam because they represent a European spirit in a body which is Arab" (16/08/80).

This statement outraged the Lebanese, but Qadhafi's view is common currency in the Maghreb. For him, Islam is not a particular society which blends natural societies together. The *umma* is necessarily and primarily ^{c}*arabiya*. Unlike the Christian church, it cannot absorb and accommodate diverse societies. If this should happen, it must be rejected, for it is unacceptable (16/08/80).

An example of this was shown by the social links established within Islam by religious brotherhoods. Their existence has not encouraged Qadhafi to reexamine his concepts. The brotherhood with which he was most familiar, the Sanusiya - he totally rejected. He once used a Bedouin proverb, "to eat like a Sanusi" in order to explain to Mirella Bianco[17]

The Green Book: its context and meaning

that he found no trace of austerity or contemplation in the Brotherhood. Yet he had certainly been influenced indirectly by the Sanusiya through its missionary activity amongst the tribes. This influence is evident in Qadhafi's views on Islam as we shall see.

His rejection of religious brotherhoods does not stem from a basically modernist attitude. In fact modernist trends in Islam usually allow for critism, so that the religion can better adapt to modern civilisation. Qadhafi rejects modern Western civilisation, despite its technological achievements, which he reluctantly accepts, specifically because of its pluralist vision of the nation.

Qadhafi's failure to deal with many questions in *The Green Book* calls for clarification.[18] Given his view of what society should be, it is hardly surprising that he has not discussed drugs, underdevelopment or terrorism. Nor need he discuss literature, poetry, or even religion and mysticism when his vision is of a Bedouin ideal of life. As far as technology and administrative organisation is concerned - data processing, agriculture and industry or bureaucracy - all this should be left to the people, who will find suitable solutions. Yet every technical choice is fraught with consequence and danger, both political and social, for today is the age of technocrats and ordinary people are hardly trained to handle such issues.

Qadhafi proposes that the population invade research departments, but the citizen cannot simultaneously be engineer, docker, politician, jurist, solicitor, garage mechanic amongst other activities, unless he has divine capacities!. In this respect Qadhafi is close to a philosophical position that democracy is the prerogative of the divine. Not only that, but those involved must also be totally equal to their rights and powers and they should share a total identity of views so that the majority be not oppressed by the minority. "The perfect society," Paul Claudel has written, "is the Holy Trinity". When idealism is pushed to the extreme, this is the inevitable consequence.[19]

A final point is that a vital omission from *The Green Book* is that it does not discuss Islam. Nowhere is there a quotation from the Quran. It is as if Colonel Qadhafi wanted to create a universal political model, and that he did not want *The Green Book* limited to Islam. Yet when he discusses education, for example, Qadhafi attacks "societies which do not allow religious knowledge to be acquired as such, societies which monopolise religious learning or those which dispense erroneous information about religion, civilisation or other people's customs..." (III, 45). In fact, this is a double criticism. First of all it is an attack on a traditional Sunni Islamic society in which the ^{c}ulama deny the revolutionary character of religion and monopolise religious learning. This impedes Qadhafi's religious ideas from penetrating such societies - even Libya itself. Secondly it refers to Westerners who have built up a completely false image of Islam and its civilisation. This particular situation has recently improved, as strenuous attempts have been made since 1974 - partly as the result of the oil crisis, no doubt, for oil supply must be an important incentive - to make Islam better understood in the West.

Yet the same criticism can also be applied to the Islamic world: Muslims who have relied on original sources to obtain an accurate knowledge of Christianity are very few. The leader of the Libyan Revolution must certainly have known this fact, as we find repeated appeals for universalism and a rejection of fanaticism in the third volume of *The Green Book*. This aspect of Qadhafi's ideology has been all too readily forgotten.

RECENT DEVELOPMENTS IN QADHAFI'S THOUGHT

The conflict with the middle class and the revolutionary committees

The absence of Islam from *The Green Book* and the presence in it of themes which are superficially similar to those of Marxism, although in reality inspired by the natural Bedouin ideal, led to a conflict with the ^{c}ulama. The conflict had been latent for a long time. It was primarily a conflict with the Sanusiya Brotherhood, the main support of the old regime. However, the order had lost its influence in Libya except in the east, around Jaghbub. The more important conflict was with the ^{c}ulama because it involved the crucial aspect of the spiritual leadership of the population at large. In Islam there is no distinction, in principle, between the spiritual and the temporal and such a conflict is, therefore, also political. The issue was a question of whether political power was to be controlled by those who dispense religious law or whether religious scholars would submit to Qadhafi's own ideology. There was another important question

The Green Book: its context and meaning

involved; would the ^{c}ulama continue to serve as intermediaries between God and man by interpreting the Quran *(tafsir al-Qur'an)*, the prophet's tradition *(sunnat al-nabi)*, and the law *(fiqh)*? If they did, they would deny any role to the political power.

Apart from the conflict with these religious groups, the practical applicaton of *The Green Book* led to a generalised conflict with the Libyan middle class - employers in industry and trade who had lost businesses under the principle of "cooperatives, not paid employees"; landlords who had lost their houses because of the slogan "houses to those who live in them"; landowners who had lost their property because of the principle "land belongs to nobody"; shopkeepers who had no shops because "trade was exploitation"; lawyers who had no work because justice should be administered by popular means; and political scientists because politics was not be considered as a science but rather as a matter concerning the people, and so on.

For this particular conflict, Qadhafi had to find devoted political allies. At first it was thought that his main support was the Army, but as early as 1970, Qadhafi sought to reduce its influence by excluding the military from government. We have seen how, in 1973, he tried governing directly through the masses *(jamahir)*. The army again lost influence in 1975 when the RCC was abolished.

Qadhafi's group of loyal supporters was reinforced in 1978-79 when the Revolutionary Committees were set up. Despite official ideology, these committees have no legal or political relationship with the people. They are neither elected nor designated - they are self-appointed or more precisely, it is their members' revolutionary ardour which makes them known. In a sense they constitute the regime's "red guards", the official ideological strike force. In general they include enthusiastic young people who leave secondary school (where *The Green Book* forms part of the curriculum) and who have no other concern but to incite the people to take power and denounce reactionary elements.

The army did not give in to Colonel Qadhafi easily. Like the rest of the middle class, it did not identify with him. After several attempted conspiracies against him - about which little is known but which took place between 1975 and 1980 - Colonel Qadhafi set up a popular militia, thus reducing the influence of the army even more. He also revealed the existence of a Free Officers Movement which had been kept secret until then and which now provides his political support base within the army. As an ultimate measure, he finally extended the revolutionary committee system to the army, where the Free Officer Movement forms its backbone.

Each of these measures was carried out in the name of the Revolution and of Islam, which is seen as a revolutionary force.

Islam as revolution

The concept of Islam as a revolutionary force is not a new theme for Qadhafi. It was an idea that he dwelt upon with particular insistence in 1978-1979, when he accompanied it with criticism of the *sunna* and became involved in an ideological and theological battle.[22]

According to Mu^{c}ammar Qadhafi, Islam is permanent revolution. The Iranian revolution came as a clear confirmation of this belief and for this reason Qadhafi did not hesitate to back it, despite the Imam Musa al-Sadr affair.[21] It has always been accepted in Islam that reform *(islah)* should be a permanent feature. For the Colonel, it is revolution *(thawra)* and not reform which should be the central concern. In a declaration to *Afrique Asie* on 5 March 1979 he said: "What should be expected from this popular revolution is that it will rely on a new modern progressive and revolutionary Islam.. I hope the Iranian revolution will develop into a *jamahiriya*." Thus the theme of Islam is always to be linked to the themes of progressivism, socialism and revolution.

It could now be argued that the leftist revolutionary and anti-imperialist themes have gained the upper hand over the Islamic ones. Whereas, in the early period of Qadhafi's thought, Islam seemed to serve Arabism, there can be no contradiction between the two for Qadhafi, since revolution springs from authentic Islam and should be achieved within and through Islam itself. In an important speech delivered at Martyrs' Square in Tripoli, on 11 November 1978, he declared: "One of the reasons for the backwardness of the Muslim world is the existence of retarded mentalities ... according to which scientific discoveries are considered as sins *(haram)*. They also present socialism to Muslims as a sin and claim that revolution and progress are also sins".

This revolution, which is to be carried out within Islam, is not directed against religion. An interview with *al-Kifah al Watani* confirms this (07/02/79). "I do not support Marx who launched a revolution against religion. On the contrary, I am calling for a revolution within Islam in order to recitfy deviations... We are struggling to eliminate hypocrites and those who exploit religion. These alone have been threatened by our religious revolution".

The attack is directed against groups such as ^{c}*ulama*, merchants, employers, particularly the influence they have on the masses. The ^{c}*ulama* have reacted, not only against Qadhafi's leftist tendencies, but also against his views on the relationship between the Quran and the *sunna*. For Qadhafi, the Quranic verse "We have omitted nothing in the complete Book" (XI, 6) makes the *sunna* unnecessary. In any case, he considers it contradictory and distorted by political quarrels over the caliphate. These views are not new for many modernists have attempted to change the *fiqh* and disregard the *shari^{c}a*, without rejecting the basic principles. The real source of ideas here is the influence of the Sanusiya, who criticised the *sunna*, accepting only a small portion of it, and rejecting the four schools of Islamic jurisprudence. The order proposed instead to reform Ibadi observance with a base synthesised from all four schools while allowing Malikism to predominate. This *ijtihad* led to the Sanusiya founder being condemned on several occasions, particularly by the well-known legal theorist Muhammad Il^{c}ish in 1842.[22]

Qadhafi's religious ideas can be seen as a continuation of the process of purification started by Ibn Taymiyya, Wahhabism, and the Sanusiya. In fact, he goes even further by completely discarding the *sunna (Khutba* at the Mawlay Muhammad mosque at Tripoli on 10 February 1978), changing the calendar (lecture on 1 December 1978) or establishing separation between politics and religion (11/07/80).

On 24 February 1979, Qadhafi told a student meeting, including students of thirty different nationalities, at Tripoli, that it was necessary to launch "a holy war against exploitation, class society and feudalism..". His dilemma is simple - given the great problems that resulted from a falsified bourgeois vision of Islam, the Muslim is unconsciously directed towards atheism. His only alternative would be "to accept those currently erroneous practices which approve of feudalism, exploitation and the control of wealth". The solution "is to be found in Islam and the Quran" - in other words, in *The Green Book*. "By following *The Green Book*, the Muslim can rise again and find a solution to his economic, political and social problems without straying from Islam and without giving up his faith."

Thus the progressive revolution laid out in *The Green Book* becomes a duty for the Muslim. On 11 November 1978 in Martyrs' Square, Colonel Qadhafi proclaimed: "Islamic revolution, which is the revolution of justice, socialism, science and the good, should be extended to all parts of the world". This proclamation of the Colonel's ultimate objective does not exclude Arab unit. On the contrary, it involves it, for now ties of kinship and blood can be put aside.

Here, the *umma ^{c} arabiya* makes way for the *umma islamiya*, or *Muhammadiya* or, preferably, the *umma thawriya* - the revolutionary community of Muslims and other progressives which is to save the world from injustice and capitalism. "The Islamic religion is the greatest of revolutions; more than that, it is a world revolution; even more than that, it is an armed revolution.. making it a duty for Muslims to become powerful, just as described in the Holy Book. This Islamic duty is an invitation to a generalised mobilisation, so that this nation *(umma)* will become strong and powerful". This is the real *jihad*.

Libya's role within this *umma* is critical and primordial. Major Jallud, Qadhafi's *alter ego*, declared on 4 March 1979: "We will not give up the leadership of the new Islamic renaissance; the *Jamahiriya* will not give up its role within the liberation movement within the Arab world, Africa and Latin America, because this role is closely linked to the 1st September Revolution.

Colonel Qadhafi often declares that "We support all popular revolutions", which clearly means that the community with which Libya identifies itself is primarily that of revolutionaries. The *umma Islamiya* is called forth every time Muslims engaged in revolution. Arabs, as such, might not fit within the concept of *umma*, but as long as they do not participate in revolution they are of no interest to Qadhafi. "This respect the Libyan people have for neighbouring Arab peoples does not allow it to carry out their revolutions for them. It is for these peoples to take on the task of their own liberation, otherwise they would not deserve emancipation and should thus be left under regimes of exploitation and slavery (02/03/81).

From this point of view, kinship should no

longer be of importance, because the revolutionary community transcends the concept of the *umma* as described in Volume III of *The Green Book*. The support given to the Iranian revolution against Iraq, although the latter is an Arab country, can be understood from this standpoint only. Clearly, when Iran was still a reactionary state, there was no need for ideological hesitation. However, it is of interest to consider Qadhafi's reaction to situations where his ideological values contradict each other - in Eritrea, Afghanistan, or even in Iran. In general, it is evident that leftist values tend to come before Islam (Afghanistan) and before Arabism (Iran, Eritrea).

Nevertheless, Colonel Qadhafi still considers kinship relations to be important. At the international seminar on *The Green Book* held in Madrid between 1 and 6 June 1980, he declared, "The solution of the Kurdish problem resides in the establishment of an independent Kurdish state on the Kurdish homeland". Thus a natural social group may claim its share of territory and become a nation, even within the Arab zone. Would not this argument serve secessionalist claims, particularly those of Berbers and Tuaregs in North Africa? No, Colonel Qadhafi would reply, since Berbers and Tuaregs are Arab. What about Jews? For Qadhafi the question is quite different, because Israel is an aggressive state in the service of imperialism.

It is clear that Qadhafi's attitude in favour of the Kurds, which is in line with the logic of *The Green Book*, makes it necessary for him to identify different specific situations. Only in this way can he limit the implications of his basic beliefs and safeguard the unity of the Arab nation. Indeed, Arabism is still of vital importance to Colonel Qadhafi.

Just as socialism has historically tolerated, or even learned to live with monolithic ideological concepts, or even as Arabism has continually wanted to be both socialist and democratic, so Colonel Qadhafi has been able to slide from one ideological formula to another without causing any surprise. He has, what is more, also been able to do this in apparent good faith and without suffering from any evident contradiction, even though such ideological approaches are mutually exclusive from both the practical and philosphic points of view.

The Green Book: its context and meaning

Notes

1. Just in terms of length, *The Green Book* only comprises about 100 pages, while the collection of Qadhafi's speeches, *Es-Sijill el-qawmi*, fills eleven volumes each of 700-1300 pages. The quotations in this study are drawn mainly from these volumes. For simplicity, references will be limited to the date of the particular speech in question.

2. In this study we have excluded questions relating to foreign policy, except when they involve important concepts such as the *umma*. We have also summarised the first two periods, as we have had the opportunity to discuss them elsewhere. Some references can be found below. On international politics see "Les chroniques de *L'Annuaire de l'Afrique du Nord*" (B Etienne).

3. On the evolution of Libyan institutions, see our political chronicle of Libya in *L'Annuaire de l'Afirque du Nord*, published by CNRS, which starts in 1970. Also see Bleuchot, H., and Monastiri, T., 1977, "L'évolution des institutions Libyennes (1969-1978)" in *L'Annuaire de l"Afrique du Nord*

4. On this period, see in particular our articles "Les fondements de l'idéologie de colonel Mu^{c}ammar al-Qadhafi" in *Maghreb Machrek* (62), March-April 1974, pp 21-27. This article also in Albergoni, G., et al, 1975, in *La Libye Nouvelle*, CNRS, Paris

5. On this concept see works by Gardet, L., in particular "L'Islam, communaute et religion", D.D.B. 1969. Recently a seminar on the concept of *umma* was held at Sassari

6. A popular movement which, within the old Arab empire, rejected Arab preeminence.

7. See Meyer, A., 1977, "Islamic Law in Libya, Analyses of Selected Laws Enacted since the 1969 Revolution", SOAS, and Atallah, B., 1974, "L'acculturation juridique dens le Nord de l'Afrique. Le cas de l'Algerie et de la Libye", *Independence et Interdependances au Maghreb*, CNRS

8. See Saade, N., 1979, *Khalil Mutran*, Lille, Chapter 1

9. This concept existed in the West as well. The Scandinavian "thing" of which traces are encountered in Iceland and Norway, and Germanic and Slavic institutions are very similar to it. In Switzerland. people still attend some *canton* assemblies in arms. In fact Switzerland claims to be a direct democracy. Cf. Siegfried, 1948, *La Suisse*

démocratie temoin, Paris, and Musset, L., 1951, *La Scandinavie au Moyen Age*, Paris

10. The appropriation of land in the interior of Libya is quite recent. It goes back to the end of the 19th century and was encouraged by the Turks.

11. See in particular, *La convivialité*, Paris, Seuil, 1973

12. "Austerity is not isolation or retirement, within oneself. For Aristotle, as for Thomas Aquinas, it is the basis of friendship" *(La convivialité*, p 13)

13. It has often been pointed out that in tribal assemblies decisions were taken by concensus. People held long discussions before reaching a decision and opposition to an idea would never appear as such, but as attempts to convince or to become convinced. This was the reason why "palavers" and "pow-wow", as described by explorers in the last century, took so much time. However, latent opposition continues to exist, waiting for an occasion to propose a wiser and more prestigious chief.

14. If, in three constituencies, each having its own congress, the first votes yes by 51 to 49 and the second also votes yes by 51 to 49, while the third votes no unanimously, the result is that the yes vote wins by two congresses to one, although we have 198 no votes (49+49+100) against 102 yes votes (51+51)

15. See Davis, J., "Theory and Practice of Non-Representative Government", in *Maghreb-Machrek* 93, September/October 1981, pp 39-55. The author discusses an election at Ajdabiyah and shows the practical contradictions of they system.

16. Struggles in Africa, and demands for regional autonomy in France (Corsicans, Bretons) or Spain (Basque country) and almost everywhere in the world tend to confirm this fact

17. Bianco. M., 1974. *Kadhafi. Messager du desert*, Paris, P 147

18. Monastiri, T., 1979, "Chronique sociale et culturelle", *L'Annuaire de l'Afrique de Nord*, analyses *The Green Book* and contains a list of its omissions

19. There is, however, one way in which a total identity of views amongst citizens can be reached. It is, unfortunately, the one which is increasingly used throughout the world - ideological indoctrination and ceaseless propaganda complemented by physical liquidation of "rejects"

20. See articles in 3 above and Meyer, A., "Islamic Law in Libya in the Era of the Green Book" in *Maghreb-Machrek* (forthcoming)
21. Head of the Shi^{c}a community in Lebanon, believed to have disappeared in Libya
22. See Delanoue, G., 1978, *Politiques et moralistes dans l'Egypte du XIXe siècle*, thesis, Paris

Acknowledgement

This article is an extended version of a paper given at a conference at the Feltrinelli Foundation, in Milan in March 1981

Chapter 11
FRONTIERS: AN IMPORTED CONCEPT: AN HISTORICAL REVIEW OF THE CREATION AND CONSEQUENCES OF LIBYA'S FRONTIERS

M. Muller

Libya's interest in the Saharan region has caused concern to her neighbours as well as to the international community in the recent past. Many African states rest uneasily within borders which neither coincide with natural nor ethnic divisions. In addition the colonial period bequeathed a considerable number of borders which to say the least are liable to ambiguous interpretation. Libya is one such state and an investigation of the history of her frontiers is important in understanding her interest in the Saharan region as a whole. The definition of 'frontiers' which we shall follow here is 'a line across which one country confronts another, a line of separation ..... even when it is only virtual and defined on the ground by boundary marks or posts located at appropriate intervals'.[1]

The 19th and 20th century literary corpus that deals with this subject, both the numerous books and articles devoted to it and the relevent diplomatic and military archives, make it clear that the concept of a frontier had a very real place within the contemporary Western European mentality. Western Europeans tried to prescribe the demarcation of such symbolic lines across the immense areas they conquered in the same terms as they used to define the differences between themselves - as English, French or Italian, for example. The significance of defining frontiers in this way was that it established a presence in a particular area that could also be used to oppose the presence there of other Europeans of different nationality and interests. At the same time, autochthonous populations were dispossessed of the space that they occupied, for the essence of the spatial and social relationships they had enjoyed there vanished and they were also divested of control over their own futures.

Frontiers - an Imported Concept

However, the number of documents given over to such matters demonstrates, at least, the persistence of this problem of frontier demarcation. It was often difficult and sometimes impossible to lay down where frontiers were to be, particularly when this implied a reality different from that contained within the conceptual confines of a military staff mentality. Resistance appeared in a variety of forms. Localised tribal revolts mirrored vast uprisings like that which blazed up throughout the Sahara in 1916 and 1917 under Sanussi influence and which succeeded for a short period in containing English, French and Italian penetration throughout North and Central Africa. There were also the *razzia-s* and counter *razzia-s* of nomadic tribes - a form of permanent unrest which made effective control of border regions rather superficial for much of the time, despite numerous reconnaissance missions, inspection trips and repressive patrols from one side of the frontier or the other. Beyond that there were vast migratory movements which involved complete families - the Fezzani, for example, moving to relatives in Tibesti after the 1st World War, as Italy started on the conquest of the Fezzan. Each of these examples demonstrates the existence and the vitality of the resistance offered by another way of life which had survived for thousands of years.

On both sides of the Sahara a series of market centres had grown up at the heads of the caravan routes. They were veritable earth-bound harbours on each side of the desert, facing each other across its vast expanse - Marrakesh, Sijilmassa, Wargla, Ghudamis, Kairwan, Tripoli and Awjila in the north, and Timbuctu, Gao, Kano and Abeche in the south. Oases in the Fezzan or in Tibesti became stopover points and transshipment or redistribution centres on these commercial routes, which count amongst the oldest roads in the world. In the 19th century the major routes linked Timbuctu to Morocco and Algeria, Kano to Ghudamis via Air, and Chad to Tripoli via Bilma and the Fezzan. They drew off slaves, gold, ostrich feathers and ivory to the Mediterranean and sent textiles, paper, tea, dates, salt and European manufactured goods south.

Alongside these vast movements of the caravans, organised by one section of the Saharan population, there were also groups who were completely sedentary or only partially nomadic. They looked after oasis agriculture and pastoral herding. Within these societies, nomadism had an essential role, both for ensuring subsistence and as a social convention.

It was quite clear that everyone involved knew the limits that existed, whether they were ethnic, tribal or geographic - the demarcation of areas of cultivation or pastureland - and they were quite prepared to fight to ensure that such limits were preserved, or even extended. At another level there was also a sentiment of allegiance to the Ottoman authorities with which other values could often be in conflict. However the limits of the *vilayat-s* were imprecise and did not necessarily imply total adhesion to the *Porte*. Both for Europeans and for the multiple and diverse Saharan populations, then, delimitation was a concept that did create a sense of belonging, an awareness of common identity, but, in each case, this awareness was completely different. European societies were sedentary and the concept of a frontier as a precise geographic line and a symbolic limit to national identity was the result of internal developments that were still evolving during the 19th century. Such an idea, expressed in this way, was completely foreign to northern Africa at the time when European colonial activity was beginning. The advent of colonialism there coincided with a major internal crisis in the caravan trade which was suffering more and more seriously from competition from sea-borne commerce. Other factors worsened the position - the abolition of slavery, the collapse of trade in ostrich feathers amongst them. Yet, despite these factors which had considerably reduced the movement of people throughout the area and had weakened the links between White and Black Africa, the Arabs, Tuaregs and Tebu in the Sahara could only survive through an integrated form of nomadism. They had to migrate, as much to acquire and redistribute products they lacked as to complement oasis vegetable produce with that from stock raising, in a rhythm that was dictated by rainfall and access to wells. Their herds provided wool, skins and meat, while camel raising also provided a means of transport.

THE HISTORICAL BACKGROUND TO LIBYA'S FRONTIERS

This brief review of the historical development of Libya's frontiers is designed to show how a concept alien to the region was introduced. It also describes the consequences of this today, for a country that gained its independence within the confines defined by colonialism, after being abandoned

Frontiers - an Imported Concept

by Italy during the 2nd World War.

Although the Ottoman Empire did exercise a degree of formal control over the provinces of Tripolitania, Cyrenaica and the Fezzan, it was not a relationship that was trouble-free, even though, in other respects, there was a feeling of allegiance and recognition of Ottoman suzerainty throughout these African provinces. A lengthy war was necessary after 1830 to re-establish direct Ottoman administration in a country where a local dynasty, the Caramanli-s, had ruled for more than a century. Furthermore, there had never been a precise delimitation of the frontier defining the region under Ottoman control. Such an idea only became relevant and began to be progressively applied as a result of increasingly numerous infringements by the French in the West and the English in the East. Piece by piece, through force of arms, vast stretches of territory were removed from the Ottoman Empire - Algeria after 1830, Tunisia fifty years later, and Egypt at more or less the same time. What was to become Libya was the last Turkish possession in Africa. The Ottoman reconquest and the removal of the Caramanli-s was a final attempt to retain a presence on the African continent.

However, by the end of the 19th century, the European powers were already ignoring the authority of the Porte, which was in turn obliged to ratify 'international treaties'. The French and the British, in 1899, signed a declaration which defined the line separating their respective zones of expansion. This line bisected the waters of the Congo and Nile river basins to latitude $11°$ North. The line between Waddai and Darfour up to latitude $15°$ north was left undetermined. Beyond that it ran along the line $24°$ east of Greenwich until it intercepted another line running south-east from the point where the line $16°$ East of Greenwich intersected the Tropic of Cancer. Despite Ottoman protests, the agreement was signed and the Italians joined it in 1902. Thus the south-east frontier of what was to become Libya was defined without any consultation being made amongst the populations involved.

In the west, the limits of the zones under French and Ottoman control were defined progressively and with great difficulty. A Franco-Turkish agreement over this delimitation was not signed until 19 May 1910. Demarcation operations on the ground began, but they were interrupted the following year

Frontiers - an Imported Concept

by the start of the Italian colonial occupation and then by the 1st World War. Since Italy was allied to Austro-Hungary by treaty, she preferred to stay neutral during 1914 since she was uncertain what benefits, if any, could be obtained from this alliance. She only decided to throw her lot in with Britain, Russia and France in 1915, and then signed an agreement with them on 25 April 1915 - the Pact of London. This required her to prosecute the war with all military means at her disposal. In return concessions were granted. Article 13 of the Pact recognised '.... the right of Italy, in principle, to request an extension to her possessions in Eritrea, Somaliland, Libya and in abutting districts of French and British colonies'. Such an extension was obtained from France in 1919, after difficult negotiations. In the 19th September 1919 Treaty, the frontier between Tunisia and Tripolitania was left unchanged thus preserving the dispositions of the Franco-Turkish treaty of 1910. With Algeria, the Tripolitanian border was moved considerably towards the west, with the specific purpose that the caravan routes linking Ghat and Ghudamis should pass solely through Italian territory. The frontier with French West Africa was also changed from the definition given in the Franco-British treaty of 1899. The new treaty provided that the frontier from Ghat to Toummo should pass along the chain of mountains that ran between the two oases, thus ensuring that the lines of direct communication would be in Italian territory.

By the end of the 1st World War, Libya had more or less the borders which were to endure until Independence on paper, even though Italy had lost control of the interior of the country and only maintained an effective presence in a few coastal towns. It took many years for her troops to occupy the country which maps had accorded to her since 1919. Once that had been done, Italy was then to attempt to extend the frontiers *inter alia* towards Tibesti. The success of this attempt was enshrined in the 1935 Laval-Mussolini Treaty, which granted Italy possession of the northern half of Tibesti, the Azou Strip, a tract of land of about 200 km deep. However, the instruments of ratification were never exchanged and the treaty had not been brought into force by 1939, when the 2nd World War began. It was never to be activated thereafter either. Although the theoretical line of the frontier was established in this way, it must be emphasised that its location often varied

Frontiers – an Imported Concept

significantly, depending on the origin of the map consulted. Some versions were deliberately left incomplete, or were even inaccurate, so that the neighbouring power should not obtain information on wells discovered during reconnaissance missions. Nor was it delimited on the ground with any precision in many places, and certain regions were still considered to bear only a 'provisional' demarcation as late as 1950. Throughout the whole of the inter-war period, up to 1939, French and Italian expeditions attempted to rectify this situation, the final attempt on the French side being the Larroque Mission.

It must also be borne in mind that, whether or not frontiers existed, nomadism continued throughout the vast area of the Sahara, as much from necessity as because of the antiquity of the links uniting distant regions together – Tibesti and the Fezzan, for example. According to an Italian study made in the 1930s, the Tebu of Tibesti went to the Fezzan for the purchase of the date harvest, which they exchanged against dried meat, skins and animals. Although the study claimed that such exchanges were on the decline, they were still observed twenty years later. The Tuaregs of the Fezzan migrated to the borders of Algeria and even into Algeria itself. They were members of tribes living in the border regions and, when they wanted to migrate, were obliged to obtain passes from the local authorities who were responsible for their administration. According to E Scarin, the groups involved were the Kel Tinrhert around Ghudamis, small fractions of noble tribes and the Imanrhasaten between Ghudamis and Awbari. The most numerous were to the south, the Quraren who were divided into both noble and vassal groups. Some Tuareg groups in the Ghat region, such as the Kel Ghat, had become sedentarised. By 1937, nomads and semi-nomads in the Fezzan represented 4393 of the 35230 inhabitants counted in an Italian census.

Commercial activity noted by the French authorities at frontier posts in the Toummo region in 1955 showed that there were comparatively few caravans, involving 120 persons moving in a north-south direction and 25 in the opposite sense. However, it is not evident that all nomads passed through the control points. It was mainly the Tebu of Tibesti who travelled from the south towards the north, on their was to collect dates in the Fezzan. This they exchanged against millet at Bilma before returning to Tibesti. The goods, transported from the north to the south, consisted of carpets, shoes, head wear, and some silver objects, sold mainly by Tunisians and Fezzani-s. Other caravans took a different path, for they ran along the south-eastern edge of the *edeyen* of Murzuq as far as the *wad* el-Kebir el-Gareh, then west of the *enneri* of Billibahar, via the Mangueni plateau and thw wells of Achelouma or Sequeddine, or the Djado oasis. All these caravans had to cross the frontiers of three different territories to complete their commercial activities - those of Niger, Chad and Libya. Books and archives amply document the persistence of these human and commercial relations, even if they were in decline, or hindered and restricted by the authorities.

The creation and imposition of frontiers was to complement other causes for the decline, among them competition from sea-borne traffic, the progressive disappearance of slavery and of trade in ostrich feathers. The technical and military means available to the Italians during the conquest and the installation of their administration within these frontiers were far superior to those of their adversaries, and they did not hesitate to use armed force. The following example clearly shows how the installation of the frontier and of full-blown colonial control ran hand-in-hand. During the second Italian attempt at conquest, just before 1930, the army built a barbed wire fence along the Egyptian border. This effectively made it impossible for the resistance movement to obtain supplies, and the measures were accompanied by an increase in the number of light patrols and frequent aerial bombardments, as well as by massive deportations of rebel tribes. Mohammed Asad describes one of the last crossings of the Cyrenaican 'frontier' by a group led by Omar el-Mokhtar. Asad heard the following description of the capture of Kufrah by the Italians from one of the few who escaped in 1931:

> They attacked us in three columns, each coming from a different direction and involving many armoured vehicles and heavy guns. Their planes flew over at low altitude, bombing houses, mosques, and palm groves. We only had a few hundred men able to bear arms, for all the rest were women, children, and the elderly. We fought back, falling back house by house, but they were too strong and, finally, only the village of al-Hawari was left in our hands. Our rifles were useless against their armoured

> cars and they crushed us. I hid myself in the palm grove... throughout the night I heard the cries of the women being raped by Italian soldiers and Eritrean *askari*. The next day an old woman found my hiding place and she brought me bread and water. She told me that the Italian general had called everyone together in front of the tomb of Sayyid Muhammad al-Mahdi. He tore a Koran to pieces before their eyes, scattered the bits on the ground, and stamped on them with his boots, saying, 'Let your bedouin prophet help you now, if he can'! Then he had all the palm trees cut down, the well destroyed and all the books in the library of Sayyid Ahmad burnt...[2]

The result of this sort of violence was that the bedouin '..no longer had access to the open territorial and human entity which, in the first half of the 19th century, extended from Surt to the Moroccan Atlas, between the plains or mountains along the littoral and the true desert'. The Sahara of 1830, in which he had been free to move around or to settle down had been broken up into separate elements.

> The boundary marks that were set up by the conquerers, who would only recognise the existence of Algerians, Tunisians, or Tripolitanians, formed frontiers that shattered the mental framework of bedouin life, even before the superiority of the occupier began to affect the economic substructure .[3]

In Libya, the first consequences of the creation of frontiers linked to the development of Italian economic, political and cultural models within them, were the growth of illiteracy and demographic decline. In 1934 the Libyan population had fallen by 13percent compared to what it had been in 1911 and indigenous economic activity was in sharp decline - Cyrenaica's main resource was ruined for nine-thenths of its lifestock had disappeard.[4]

In the longer term, these results were to lead to a paradox, for the concept of a frontier took geographic roots. Once the occupiers had left, the framework they had created remained more or less unchanged. Two questions then arose - how were the populations living in the frontier zones to be treated, and, what consideration would be given to the requirements that still remained for nomadism, and the specific problems of nomads?

THE FIRST INDEPENDENT STATE OF AFRICA

For Libya, the 2nd World War was a period of destruction; it became the arena in which the German, Italian, English and, in a minor capacity, the French armies faced each other. There is an abundant literature that describes this 'desert war', 'war without hate', 'epic', with the famous battles at Bir-Hakeim, El Alamein, and Tubruq. Libyans hardly appear in this literature at all, and it seems as if their country simply existed to provide a battleground for the opposing armies. Even to-day, books appear every year dealing with this subject, in response to evident demand. A semantic study of the mythology of the 'desert hero' which received its apotheosis during the 2nd World War, would no doubt yield interesting results. As a random example consider this excerpt from General de Gaulle's preface to General Ingold's 1943 book, *The Epic of Leclerc in the Sahara*. In it he writes:

> In the centre of Africa, physically separated from their homeland, all the better to serve it, soldiers demonstrated those qualities that distinguish the sons of a great nation; the taste for risks, the cult of sacrifice, a sense of honour, acceptance of discipline, methodical effort, a determination to succeed...'[5]

The fruit of these battles was a new conquest, for the struggle for liberty from an invader in France took on a different significance in Africa. In fact it became what it had been during the 1st World War - an extension of colonial possessions by force of arms. By 1943, Italy and Germany seemed as if they would probably lose the war. In the same year the Yalta agreements were signed and divided the post war world into spheres of influence. General de Gaulle ends his preface as follows:

> Yet, because they wanted to fight and win, occupied France has been able, despite all to bring a brilliant contribution to the battle for Africa. She has fought in Eritrea, Ethiopia and Libya. She has conquered in the Fezzan. Children of France, dream that one day you will be one of Leclerc's own, read this book and learn what a free French spirit is worth. Algiers, 1st October 1943.

The Leclerc column, which started out from Chad in 1941, took the initiative in annexing the Fezzan. General Leclerc handed over its administration to the Algerian colonial authorities on 1 September 1943.

Frontiers - an Imported Concept

Once the war was over, it was decided at international level that Libya was to become independent before the end of 1951. Until then Tripolitania and Cyrenaica were to remain under British administration, while France would administer the Fezzan. According to the report made to the UN by the commission responsible for preparing the path to independence, under the control of a Dutchman, Adrian Pelt, the Fezzan was:

> administered by French military authorities using Fezzani functionairies as intermediaries. The territory of the Fezzan was under the control of three local administrations and two ministries in Paris. On the ground there was a resident at Sebha whose authority extended throughout the Fezzan, except for the region of Ghat-Serdeles which, from an administrative point of view, is attached to the military region in southern Algeria, and the district of Ghadames which is attached for administrative purposes to the military region in southern Tunisia. In France, two authorities divide matters relating to the Fezzan between themselves - the Ministry for Foreign Affairs for matters which relate to relations between the Fezzan and the exterior, and the Ministry of the Interior for everything to do with the relationships of the Fezzan to neighbouring French territories and for the internal administration of the territory.[6]

As far as the question of frontiers was concerned, the General Assembly of the United Nations recommended on 15th December 1950 that:

> The frontier of Libya with French territories, in so far as it has been delimited by international agreement, shall be delimited after Libya has acceded to independence by means of negotiation between the Libyan government and the French government, aided, should either party request it, by a third person chosen by them or, in case of a failure to agree, by the Secretary-General.

During the years that followed, France tried to make sure that its own interest prevailed, attempting, for example, to retain the Ghat region, basing her argument on the fact that the same ethnic group inhabited both sides of the frontier, a fact that she only recently seemed to have discovered since, when the Italians were her neighbours, France had always argued for the limitation of nomadism. In another area, France used the argument that the Laval-

Mussolini accords of 1935 had never been ratified.
This enabled her to refuse to include the north
Tibesti region within the frontiers of independent
Libya. Finally, she requested the possession of the
Fezzan, or of certain parts of it - as was illustrated by her policy of dividing it amongst three different territorial administrations - in the interests
of preserving the French Empire in Africa and on the
grounds of the need to preserve control of rapid and
direct routes that would link Tunis to Chad (eg
piste imperiale/imperial route No. 5). Air bases at
Sabhah, Ghat and Ghudamis were also claimed to be indispensible in providing air cover for the Saharan
regions of Algeria and Tunisia. Between 1951 and
1954 France persuaded the newly independent state of
Libya, ruled by the monarchical regime of Muhammad
Idris who had returned from exile to renew previous
agreements and permit the continued maintenance of
air bases in the Fezzan. However, after 1954, the
Libyans were no longer prepared to tolerate this
situation and, after considerable difficulties, the
two governments reached agreement. The treaty, signed
on 10th August 1955 by Maurice Dejean for France and
by Mustapha ben Halim for Libya, was to last for
twenty years and stipulated that:
> The French government undertakes to withdraw
> its military forces at present in the Fezzan.
> The evacuation will be completed within a period
> of 12 months after the entry into force of this
> treaty and, at the latest, by 30th November
> 1956. (Article 1).

For its part, the Libyan government pledged that,
after the departure of the French troops stationed
in the Fezzan:
> It would ensure the occupation of this region
> and the execution of any activity of a military
> nature that the circumstances might require
> would be performed by exclusively Libyan troops.

This article also referred to the English and
American military missions that were in Cyrenaica
and Tripolitania. The Fezzan was not to fall within
their sphere of influence:
> The Libyan government will favourably consider..
> requests made to it by the French government
> for the passage of French military convoys des-
> tined for, or originating from Chad along
> route No.5.

Other conditions in this special convention, which
was attached to a treaty that was essentially one
of good neighbourliness, made it clear that although
French military forces would have to be withdrawn,

their influence, especially in respect of military matters would continue. Amongst the specific conditions attached to the treaty, the two governments also undertook to: '... provide facilities for the transhumance of nomads from tribes that traditionally migrate across the Algerian-Libyan frontier...' This was the first time that concern for the problems of nomads had actually been enshrined in a treaty, and it occurred at a time when France had a dominant role in discussions. As far as the frontiers themselves were concerned, they were defined in Annex 1 of the Treaty by reference to the international agreements of 1899 (the Anglo-French Agreement),1902 (the Italo-Franco-British Agreement), 1910 (the Franco-Turkish Treaty) and the 1919 agreement (which followed on from the Pact of London of 1915). However, there was no reference to the 1935 Laval-Mussolini Accords. France thus retained control of the Azou Strip, which was to stay as an integral part of Chad: 'A mixed commission will be charged with the delimitation of the frontier wherever this has not yet been done and wherever one of the two governments feels it to be necessary'.

Thus political independence and sovereignty were achieved between 1951 and 1955 but much still remained to be done to achieve genuine independence that Libyans themselves would consider satisfactory and complete. There was an active sense of solidarity and common purpose that extended across frontiers, both with Tunisia and even more strongly with Algeria. This was evident in the supply of arms and aid to the Algerian resistance during the struggle between 1956 and 1962. Initial oil prospecting expeditions encountered hostility from local people, and several expatriate camps were attacked. At the same time, because the French authorities feared the consequences of the war in Algeria, the military commands in French West Africa, French Equatorial Africa, and Algeria were coordinated. This was done despite reluctance shown by the command centres in each territory, for they each feared they would lose their freedom of action.

THE PROBLEM OF FRONTIERS IN AFRICA

Independence came to the countries of North Africa between 1956 and 1962. It came more slowly to some states to the south of the Sahara , and still has not come to South Africa. Those states that have achieved independence have either been granted it

or fought for it within the colonial frontiers that
were established long before, as we have seen in the
case of Libya. These frontiers also formed the
framework in which nationalist sentiments which
were to give rise to independent nation-states developed, in countries such as Libya, Tunisia, Egypt,
Algeria, Chad or Niger. Such sentiments have become
a reality and find a profound response amongst the
populations to which they apply. Nonetheless, their
existence has not prevented an awareness of the
existence of other links, which can often be in
conflict with nationalism, links involving cultural,
social, regional, ethnic (berber-Arab, nomad-sedent-
ary, etc), or even political or ideological (Arab
Nation, or Third World) features. Despite these
features, however, the frequent border disputes
between independent African states demonstrates that
the national context is the primary means of identification.

However, it is frequently the case that the
borders as drawn are highly unsatisfactory: 'Forty
four percent of African frontiers follow meridian
lines or parallels, 30 per cent are based on geometrical
procedures using rectilinear lines or curves and only 25
per cent are natural frontiers, based on waterways,
lakes or mountains'.[6]

In response to this phenomenon, two attitudes
currently prevail in Africa. The first is that proclaimed during the First Panafrican Conference held
at Accra in December 1958: 'Barriers and artificial
frontiers laid down by the imperialists to divide
African peoples to the detriment of Africans themselves must be abolished or modified'.

However, it is extremely difficult to put this
into practice and becomes a source of conflict because each attempt to achieve it is made extremely
dangerous by, on the one hand, national sentiment
and the class interests of ruling groups in the
states involved, and the frequently contradictory
influences of the powers (both capitalist and
socialist) that support them, on the other. Political
independence is not a guarantee of full independence
and many bonds of dependence remain, among them
economic, financial, technical and military ties.
In the case of Libya alone even after the French
troops in the Fezzan had effectively withdrawn in
1957, there were still British military bases at
Darnah, Barqah, Benghazi, Misuratah, Al Khums,
Tarhunah, Tajurah, Tripoli and Sabratah, and American
bases at Darnah, Benghazi, Misuratah, Wheelus Field
(a military base close to Tripoli), Tripoli, Gharyan,

Frontiers - an Imported Concept

Jado, Sabratah, Zuwara and Nalut. These concessions were granted by the Libyan government in return for financial aid that formed an essential part of the national budget, until oil wealth overturned this vision of Libya as a desert state and therefore a necessarily dependent one. It was only after the overthrow of the monarchy in September 1969 that Libyans were able to take over control of their own natural wealth and ensure the removal of British and American troops; processes that were undertaken in succeeding years. Colonel Qadhafi's attempts at the union of states and the destruction of the concept of frontiers first tried out with Egypt and Tunisia, has not been successful, and relations between the Maghribi states are not good. Does this then mean - and this is the second attitude adopted by some African states - that frontiers are to be treated as sacrosanct? Are artificial frontiers better than fratricidal conflict? This was the position taken up by the Organisation of African Unity in 1963 and by the Heads-of-State of the Non-Aligned Countries at Cairo in 1964:

> The countries taking part in this conference, having, for the most part, achieved their national independence after years of struggle, reaffirm their determination to oppose by all the means at their disposal any attempt to compromise their sovereignty or to violate their territorial integrity. They undertake to respect the frontiers in the form they had at the moment when the states involved achieved independence'.[7]

Since then, events have frequently contradicted this statement of principle. Two problems overlap here. The first is that of a border policy which is often artificial and the cause of conflict, and the second is that of the dependence of states on the providers of financial support. This is a dependence that Libya has been largely able to avoid because of her oil resources.

This analysis sheds a different light on the current attempt at unity between Libya and Chad. It is, perhaps, an attempt to overcome the colonial heritage which, in Tibesti, divides a Muslim and Tebu community. There is also, no doubt, a Libyan desire to prevent the gap left by the departure, at Chadian insistence, of French troops, from turning into a means of coercion by neighbouring states, all dependent in differing degrees on American or European allies, particularly as far as their policies towards the Third World and Arab states is concerned. It corresponds to a conscious desire to offer a third way, particulary for under-developed countries, which would be the beginning of the non-alignment and a re-ordering of the balance of power.

Notes

1. Larousse du XXe Siecle
2. Asad, Muhammad, *Le chemin de la Mecque*, Paris Fayard, 1974, p 308
3. Marel, Andre, *Les confins saharo-tripolitains de la Tunisie (1881-1911)*, 2 vols., Paris PUF, 1965, Vol II, p 355
4. Souriau, Christiane, 'La Libye moderne', in *La Libye nouvelle rupture et continuité*, CRESM, 1975, p 144
5. Ingold, General, *L'epopée Leclerc au Sahara*, Paris, 1944, Preface by General de Gaulle, pp IX-X
6. United Nations *Annual Reports of lthe Commissioner of the United Nations in Libya, prepared in consultation with the Council for Libya*, Lake Success, New York, 1950, p 9, para 58. Similar documents also exist for 1951
7. Boutros-Ghali, *Les conflicts de frontières en Afrique (Etudes et documents)*, Paris, 1973, p 10
8. Ibid.

Frontiers - an Imported Concept

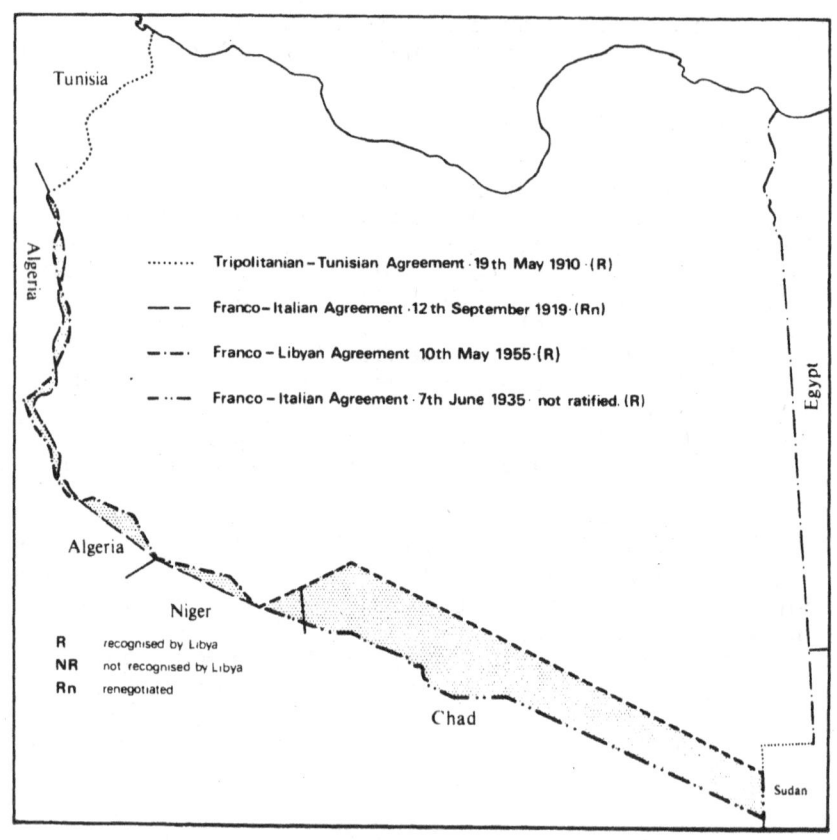

Figure 8   Border Agreements and Disputed Borders

INDEX

administration, government 124-6,136,140,145
Agip Libya 44
Agostini 104,108
agriculture before oil 11-14, 94
agricultural development
  projects costs of 21
  exports 14,18
  policy, twentieth century 25,32-3,55,63
  production 15,17,32, 99,140 see al Kufrah
  strategies 20-2, 51
  system 5-6 see farming, land use, oases
aid, foreign 13,94,124,139
  United Kingdom 13
ait 105
Ajadabiyah 111,113,116
el Alamein 173
Amal, oilfield 44
Amara Dam 105
amenity use 19
Amerada Hess 43
Amoco 45
Amoseas 44,46
aquifers, coastal 30,32
  see groundwater
Arab nationalities 129,141-2
  unity 130-2, 140
Arabian Gulf Exploration Company 44,46
Arabism 141-3,146,158,161
arboriculture 6
archaeology 3,3,8

settlement 7
army 123,140,157-8
Abu Ateiffel, oilfield 44
Atlantic Richfield 43
Augila, oilfield 43

Baghdad OPEC meeting 39
Bahi, oilfield 43
Bani Walid 3-5,68
Bank, Real Estate and Industrial 56,58
baraka 105
barley 4,6
Barth, Heinrich 3,4
batn 104
bayt 107,105
bedouin 105, 110-118,144,147 -151,155-6,172
Benghazi 22,28,56,63,94, 95,103,122,177
Berbers 103,154
Bin Gashir 33
Bir Hakeim 173
boats, fishing 86-88
border areas 10, see frontiers
Bovill, E W
Bregah 61, 64-66
British Government 107-8 121-2, 128,139,166,168
  Military Administration 10,174
  Petroleum 44,46
Brogan, O 4

funerary structures 6
gas exports 46,48,61
  natural 37,41-48,62,65
  pipelines 44-46,64
  reserves 42
qasr 5
Gefara 28-34
  water use 21
Ghirza 4-6
Ghudamis, small-scale irrigation project 11,170
Gialo, oilfield 43
Goodchild, R G 4
Government, federal 122-4 129,131
  intervention 14,16
  provincial 122,123
Greece 75,81
Green Book, The 19,137-164
Gross Domestic Product,GDP 17,51,58,60,93-4,99
Gross National Product,GNP 76
groundwater, fossil 28-9, 32,34
  renewable 28-9,32
gsur, agricultural system 4-7
Gulf Oil 41
Hamada al-Hamrah zone 41
Hamilton, J 113
haram 105
Hispanoil 45
Hofra oilfield 44
al Khalij 41
Hornemann,F 107
housing 16
Hunt 44
hydrocarbon resources 41-6 48-52 *see* gas,oil
hydrogeologists 30,32

Idris al Sanusi, King 121- 132,139-40,147,175
  Emir Sayyid 107
import substitution 67,69
income 38,94
independence 121-2,124,128-9 132,167,169,174,176-8
industrial exports 62-3,65
industrialisation 51,55,145
  see factories,oil industry

industry, fishing 73-90
  heavy 55,58,61-7,69
  light 55,64,67-8,69
  petrochemical 40,51,55 58,62,65-6,99
  secretariat of 57,64,68
  small-scale 58
infrastructure 64,69,93,96 145
Institute for Land Reform and Reclamation 18
Intisar, oilfield 43,50
investment 14,16-7,20, 30 56-59,64,66,77,89,93-9
irrigation 13,17,19,26,30, 34,117
  see also Ghudamis, groundwater, al Kufrah, water
  private sector 30-1,33
  projects,large scale 20
  sprinkler 31
  trickle 34
Islam 138,141-6,154-60
Israel 139-40,144,161
Italian authorities 10,121, 140,148,171-2
  colonial administration 10,16,169
  colonial agricultural patterns 11
  farms 12,18
  settlers 12,74-5,139
Italo-Libyan Accords 12, 18
Italy 75,166,168

Jabal al Akhdar 28,109
Jadaydah 19
Jaghbub 109,110
Jews 103,161

Abu Kammash 61,66
Karamanli,Yusaf 107
al Khums
kinship 105,160-1
al Kufrah 10,17-8,21,109-11

Labdah 62
labour 19,20,68,151
land clearance 15
  ownership 19,118,127

Index

capital, repatriation of 12
  surplus 55,69
caravans 108-9,166,169-171
Catalana de Gas, Spain 48
cistern capacities 7,116
citrus farms 19,30-1,34
coastal districts 10,28,32,
  63,73,91,169
colonialism 148,165,167
colonization, Italian 15
communications 6
communist(s) 129,130,141,143
Conoco 43
consultants, foreign 15,32,
  64,77,95 see hydrogeologists
continental shelf, Mediterranean 41,73,76,80,81
cooperatives 17,157
credit 12,16,17,19
cultural diversity 103-120
Cyrenaica 11,12,15,79,103-125,168,172-5

Dahra, oilfield 43
Darnah 56,62,68,95,177
Defa, oilfield 43
demand for foodstuffs 19
democracy 138,140,146-151 155,161
development, agricultural 9-24,25,33
  economic 1-100
  industrial 55-71
  infrastructure 16
  oil industry 37-54
  rural 15
  social 16,101-120
Economic and Social Transformation, First Plan of 58
  Second plan of 58
Edjele, Algeria 41
education 77,104,126,129,131 140,148,152,155
Egypt 29,104,109,128,130,141-145, 168,171,177,178
elections 125,126,131,150
Elf-Aquitaine 45
employment 19-21,55,59,62,75, 88,140 145,151-2
enclosure, land 19

ENI, Italy 45,48
environmental problems 9
epigraphic evidence 6
erosion 7
Esso Sirte 43,45-6,61
Esso Standard 41-2,45-6
estate development 15
Evans-Pritchard,E E 106-107,110,114
expenditure, agricultural 18
exports see agricultural exports, development, oil industry, industrial expoerts, oil
Exxon 43

fascism 148
factories 31,56,67-8,77
Fanon, F 30
farming, arable 7,9
  see land use
  commercial 13
  full-time 21
  mixed 6
  part-time 16
  rainfed 28
  Roman 7,8
  small-scale oasis 13
farmland, prices of 16
farms, private 20
federation 122,124,126
Fezzan 11,34,63,103-4,107-11,121-2,166-8,170-1, 174-5,177
fish catches 74-6,83
fishermer number of 87
fishing, types of 79-86
five year plans 15,17,30, 56,77,94-7
FAO 75,85
food production 34,58
  see also agriculture, farming, irrigation
Forbes, Rosita 109
foreign exchange 20,49,51, 52,55,69
  policy 125-8,144
Franco-British Treaty 169
Franco-Turkish Treaty 168
frontiers 165-180

148,157
land redistribution 21
  tenure 32
land use 10
  arable 9,10
  see farming,arable
  forest 10
  grassland 10
  intensive 4
  orchard 4
  pasture 10,148,167
  prehistoric 4
  scrubland 10
  wastelands 10
  urban 10
  language 104
Laval-Mussolini Treaty 169, 174-6
law 144,152,156
Leclerc column 173
Leptis Magna 3
Libya, Southern 19
  Western 12,19,20,91
Libyan-American Reconstruction Commission 13
  Development Council 13
  Fishing Company 81
  General Petroleum Corporation(Lipetco) 44-5
  National Oil Co (LNOC) 43,46,48,51
  Public Development and Stabilisation Agency 13
limitanei 4,6
liquified natural gas (LNG) 45-6,61-2,65
livestock 4,6,19
  grazing 7,9

Maghreb, The 10,154,178
Majid, oilfield 45
Malta 75,84
Marathon 43
marine productivity 78-79
al Marj 11,104
market, European 63,69
  international 38,65
  participation by Libyan farmers 14
  Roman coastal 6
  centres 166

Marsa al Breqa, oil terminal 42-3,45
Marsa Hariga 45
Marsa Sabratah 77
Marxism 143,156,159
el Mehdawi, M 56,68
migration 21,117,167,170
  rural-to-urban 16,19,115
military bases, foreign 140, 175,177-8
Minerals Law of 1953 37
Ministry of Agriculture 13,33
  Industry 56
  National Economy 14
  Planning and Development 14
Misuratah 12,28,43,46,56,61, 63-4,66,177
Mobil-Gelsenberg 44,46
monarchy 19
Abu Moosa, islands 44
Muntassa, Omar 64
Murphy 45
Murzuq 45
Mussalla, oilfield 45
Nafoora, oilfield 44
Nasa 15,16,17
Nasser, President 127-30, 138-141,145
  oilfield 45
nation, concept of 152-156
National Assembly 103,121-2
National Public Organisation for Industrialisation 57
nomads 12,148,167,170,172, 174,176-7

Oasis Oil Company 43,46
oases 17,109,111-2,166-7,169
Occidental Libya 43-4,46,50
offshore zone 41,45,50,75
oil, conservation of 40,50
  exploration 40-1,45,50-1 139,176
  impact on agriculture 14, 18,28
  reserves 42,49,50,62,178
  companies, international 38-9,40,51,126,139
  companies, nationalisation

Index

of 39,42-5
consumption 36,46-51
exports 12,14,20,38,42-51, 55,61-64
industry, development of 37-54
oil pipelines 42-4
production 36-40,46-50, 62,127,129,131
western 41,139
Opec 38-41,46,49,50
Ora, oilfield 44
Ottoman authorities 10

Pact of London 169,176
Pallas,P 27,28,33
pastoral-shifting cultivation 9
pastoralism 3,6-7,106,118
Perspective Plan 21
Petroleum Laws 38,39
Phillips 45
planning 16,20
police force 123,140
political ideology 128-131
institutions 122-5,145
policies 125-8,144
pollution 82
population 7,63-4,68,74,94 104,106,108,112-4,121-4, 155-6,165-8,172,177
private sector 15,17,20,57
see irrigation
production to reserves ratio 20,50
provincialism 129
public sector 57
utilities 16
pumps, diesel 17,30,33

qabila 105-6,111
al Qadhafi, Colonel Mu'ammar 17,19,61,137-164
Qasar Banat 6
al Qassabat 103
Quran 143,155,157,159,172

Raguba 43,45
Ras Lanuf 44-5,61,64,67
regional plans, 1981-2000
revolution, agricultural 31

cultural 138,145,158,160
Libyan 32,29,95,138,143, 145,153,160 see Arabism, Green Book, al Qadhafi
Revolutionary Command Council 57,141,146,157-8
Riah 42
Robb, E 11
Roman Empire, frontier defence 4
Romano-Libyan Period 2,4
Rowland, F 11
rural inertia 16

Sabhah 22
Sabratah 3,83,177-8
Sadat, President 145
Sanusi 106,109-10,122-5,154-6, 166
Sarir, projects 10,18,21,34, 45,64
Saudi Arabia 65,67
Sawfaggin, wadi system 3,4
Sayigh, Y A 56
Scolart, Professor 75
Serbetis 85
settlement, prehistoric 3
small farm 18
system, Roman 5
Sharif, Muhammad 109
Shell 43,45
es Sider, oil terminal 43
Siwa 109
Socal 44
social organsiation 103-120
socialism 129,141-6,148-9, 151-2,158,161,177
Sogreah 87,88
sponge fishing 84-6,88
subsidies 17,19,22,31,51,64
Suez crisis 38
Surt Basin 41-2,61,64,66,77
Gulf of 42,46,79,103,140
Suwani bin Yadim 68,177

Tajurah 68,177
Tarhunah Jabal 3,18,177
Tazerbo 34
Tebu 104,170
Tehran Agreement, 1971 39
Texaco 44

Tubruq 68,77,95,139,173
trade, trans-Saharan 107-10
Transformation Plan, 2nd 55
transport 63,92-100,167,171
tribes 104-8,111-5,121,139
   146-151,166-7,170,176
Tripoli 22,28,30,33.50,
   56,63,68,75,77,86,94-
   95,103,107,109,130,158,
   177
Tripoli Agreement,1971 39
Tripolitania 3,11-2,15,
   17,79,82,103-4,108,110,
   117,121,125,168-9,172,
   174-5
Tuareg 103
Tunbs, islands 44
Tunisia 79,81,143,168-72,
   174-8
Turks 109,121,167,168

Umm al Gawbi, State Oil
   Company 44
uncultivable lands 19
United Nations 13,122,
   174
United States of America
   129,139

Valleys Survey, Unesco
   Libyan 2,4,5
vines, cultivation of 6

Wadi Ki'am Estate 13
Wadi Nufayd 6
wadi walls 7
wadis 3-6
wastelands 9
water see groundwater
   desalinised 34
   conservation policies
   32
   in agriculture 23-35
   see also agriculture,
   development agricult-
   ural, irrigation, farming
   resource use 25,26,28,
   33,51,63-4,116
   resources, depletion of
   17

shortage 19,106
use, regional 27
use, type of 27
Wintershall 45
World War, First 173
World War, Second 10,168,
   173
World War, post-Second 75
   76,121

Yalta Agreements 173

Zagaar, Abdessalam 40
Zamazam, wadi system 3,4
al-Zamil, Abdulaziz 67
Zawiyah, oil refinery 41,
   45,61,123
Zelten oilfield 42,45-6
   see also Nasser
Zliten 62,83
Zuwarah 61,77,85,88,110-1
   178
Zuwaytinah 46
Zuwaytinah, oil terminal
   43

186